PEACE
CORPS
WRITERS

THROUGH THE EYES
OF MY CHILDREN

The Adventures of a Peace Corps Volunteer Family

*Our Peace Corps Family: Paul, Nancy, Delia (our maid) Peter,
Daniel, Frances, and Matthew (standing) in the Philippines, 1972*

Frances L. Stone

A Peace Corps Writers Book.

An imprint of Peace Corps Worldwide.

FIRST PEACE CORPS WRITERS EDITION, 2012

THROUGH THE EYES OF MY CHILDREN:
THE ADVENTURES OF A PEACE CORPS FAMILY

For more information, contact peacecorpsworldwide@gmail.com

Peace Corps Writers and the Peace Corps Writers colophon are
trademarks of PeaceCorpsWorldwide.org

ISBN-10: 1935925075
EAN-13: 9781935925071

Library of Congress Control Number: 2011942583
CreateSpace, North Charleston, SC

Cover Photo: Daniel, Nancy, Peter, and Vicky (student) and Carabao.
Philippines 1973

For my children
Who are this book

– and –

My grandchildren - you know who you are
Twinkles Toes
Princess
Ladybug
Pumpkin
Peanut
Jesse, Michael and Garrick
And of course little Catherine

Love you all,
Rainbow Grammy

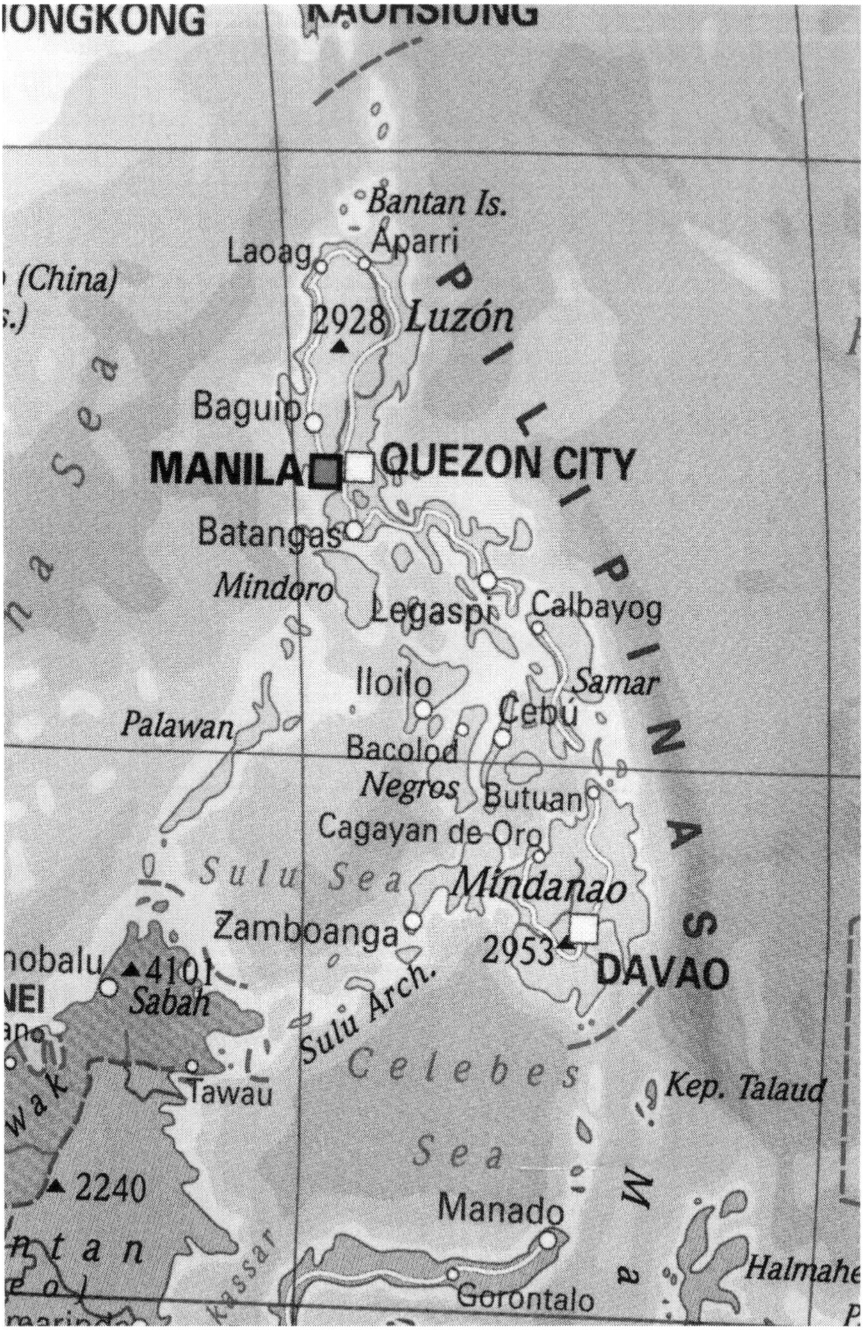

Bantan Is.
Laoag
Aparri
(China)
2928
Luzón
PILIPINAS
Baguio
MANILA
QUEZON CITY
Sea
Batangas
Mindoro
Legaspi
Calbayog
Samar
Iloilo
Cebú
Palawan
Bacolod
Negros
Butuan
Cagayan de Oro
Sulu Sea
Mindanao
Zamboanga
2953
DAVAO
4101
Sabah
Sulu Arch.
Tawau
Celebes Sea
Kep. Talaud
2240
Manado
Gorontalo

TABLE OF CONTENTS

Foreward

I had the good fortune to be Country Director in the Philippines during the years that Frances Stone and her family were Peace Corps Volunteers there.

Those years, the 1970s, were the only time that entire families could join the Peace Corps and serve in-country together. During that time instead of the single volunteers, or the occasional married couple, the Peace Corps and the United States as a whole were represented by family units: mom, dad, and any number of children. It is hard to exaggerate how important these families were to creating the strong cross-cultural connections that are so vital to the accomplishment of the Peace Corps mission. Like many other countries with Peace Corps programs, the Philippines is very family oriented. Sometimes it seems as if it is the presence of children that holds the society together. In such an environment, the Stone family, with their four children, had a cultural adventure that demands a retelling. In this book Frances Stone has met that demand and more.

The Stone children's years in the Philippines were filled with the kind of adventures that will captivate young minds. They climbed mountains, felt the effects of typhoons and floods, ate strange and exotic foods, struggled with a new language, endured the discomfort of always being the center of attention, made friends with people who were at once different from them yet also very much like them, and discovered that life can be rich and rewarding even for people lacking the material goods Americans take for granted. The adventures themselves make for exciting reading, but equally important, is the way they introduce young readers to daily life in that Asian country. Especially in today's world, knowing about and identifying with other cultures is a fundamental aspect of becoming a fully prepared citizen of our shrinking world.

The Philippines is an exciting and exotic land, where several Asian cultures have joined to create a new and vibrant culture that is unique to itself. One finds elements of the indigenous Filipino cultures inter-mixed with Chinese, Malayan and – oddly enough – American influences, all of which are combined in a way that challenges the understanding of every visitor.

Frances and her family did not remain simply visitors. They entered into the life of their neighbors in every possible way. The results are revealed dramatically in her stories, which are told in the voices of her children. Together the stories capture the remarkable hospitality of the Filipinos, the glorious natural beauty of the countryside, and the sometimes utter incomprehensibility of another way of life. The Peace Corps life at its best is filled with the kind of satisfactions that create wonderful lifelong memories. Of course, given the very nature of the way Peace Corps Volunteers live, there are also challenges that test one's fortitude and resolve. Stone's account leaves no doubt that both types of challenges existed, but in the end she makes it clear that for her, her husband and especially the children, the satisfactions carried the day.

Young readers will find these stories fascinating because some of them are mighty adventures, others are the stuff that makes for fantasy daydreams, and all are told from an age-appropriate viewpoint. But equally important – maybe even more important – the readers will meet another culture and begin to understand it: a culture like their own in some respects, and very unlike it in others.

Frances Stone's telling of the stories from the children's point of view is superb. She has captured their voices in a manner that reflects the sometimes unfettered, sometimes judgmental, sometimes wondrous way the young see the world. Once in a while we do sense the voice of the mother as she interjects a comment or two, but this just adds to the book's charm.

Although the book is aimed specifically for the youth market, I will venture a guess that many older readers, particularly parents wondering just how adventurous they can make the lives of their own children, will be captivated by it. Maybe even to the point of scheduling a trip to the Philippines for their own families.

P. David Searles

Peace Corps Staff, 1971-76

Acknowledgements

Through the Eyes of My Children came about because of over 100 letters I wrote during my family's stay in the Philippines for two years as a Peace Corps Volunteer family. It was in these pages that I found the voices of my four children, who were also considered volunteers, and I knew they had a story to tell that was different than the stories of adult volunteers. I could also hear their voices speaking through me to young adult readers

It took years for this story to be told simply, because it took years to raise four children and to work on our farm, among many other activities and obligations. But the time finally came and it took off with the help of a course in writing for publication with the Long Ridge Writers Group, under the direction of my instructor Tom Hyman. He guided me for two years and when the course was finished, but not the book, he strongly encouraged me to carry on. Thank you, Tom.

It was obvious to me that I would need another person outside my family to latch onto to keep me moving forward and remind me I had something of value to offer. I found John Barstow right here in Middlebury, Vermont, and he opened his mind and heart to my endeavors. Our time together, going over different essays, kept me moving forward until the day came when he told me I was ready to find a publisher. Thank you, John.

Then in stepped David Searles, Peace Corps Director in the Philippines when we were serving there. I even found David in my many letters, mentioning how supportive he was of our family while we were there. David has become my real ally, having been there himself and knowing what it was like for volunteers in the Philippines -- even writing his own book. He jumped right on board when he heard I was doing the book in the voices of the children. He read many of my essays and, like so many other people, kept me on track and supported my ideas. I was thrilled when he said he would be pleased to write a foreword to the book. Thank you, thank you, David for your support and faith in my work.

It was David who brought to my attention the fact that Peace Corps Worldwide was working with Peace Corps Volunteers who wanted to publish memoirs of service. I knew this was the way I wanted to go, because I wanted Peace Corps Writers emblem on my book as a token of my belief in Peace Corps.

Ann Cooper introduced me to the world of editing. I gasped as I saw all those red lines, cross-outs, and suggestions as I started going over the essays she was helping me fix. It was hard letting go of words that seemed so essential to me. But, I soon learned and understood what it was all about and found the necessary changes enhanced my book, while keeping the voices of my children. It was still my book-- and theirs. My appreciation and respect for Ann's help in going through this work with me can't be expressed adequately in words. So I'll keep it simple: Thank you, Ann.

My other supporters – family and friends – kept reminding me that I did indeed have a story worth telling. They were willing to listen to some of the early drafts and my ideas, and to share their own. I was truly pleased when Nancy said she would write the introduction; an honor in itself since she is a terrific writer in her own right. The willingness of all four of my children, now grown and with lives of their own, to write and think about where they now are in their lives, certainly added to my respect and love for them as the individuals they are. But by far, the most fun was with the grandchildren. They read parts of the book, being fascinated by the story, and by reading about their own parents as children at a very unusual time in their lives. Their input as "little editors"--Emily, Moira, Chloe, and Nathan-- was most helpful in keeping me on track in attempting to write in the words of children for readers like them. As we know, grandchildren can be an inspiration, a reminder of the simple joys and wonders of life. They may never have the chance to be Peace Corps Volunteers, but again who knows. I do know that reading these stories will broaden their world and minds a little bit more, as I hope it will also do for others.

INTRODUCTION

The Fabric of My Skin

— by —

Nancy L. Stone

I have a childhood memory. I remember an outdoor event I attended with my family that included the butchering and roasting of a pig. I remember the dark blues of evening cool against my sun-heated skin. If I close my eyes, I can see the sparks, from the fire pit where the pig roasted, flying into the darkness like fireflies on a summer evening. I eagerly waited with the other children to see who would get the pig's tail. I don't know why I got it, but I distinctly remember the visceral satisfaction of crunching on the greasy tail and the happiness that I felt being in the company of friends and family on what was for me a perfect night.

The memory of that night in the Philippines is woven into the fabric of all my childhood memories. I think of my memories as being my skin, memories that are patched together and sewn into the fabric that is the whole me. The night of the pig roast, we were probably the only white family in attendance. I played with my brothers and Filipino friends, in the gathering darkness, without thinking about being in a different country, learning about a different culture, eating new foods, learning Filipino dances and songs, or wearing a dress in traditional Filipino style. I was only making friends and forming childhood memories that are forever stitched into the fabric of my skin.

These types of experiences and the forming of these common memories erase prejudice and unite us into one people. We can read an article in a magazine, watch the evening news, surf through video clips on YouTube, view documentaries, and read books. However, we are only voyeurs of the experience, separated from the experience by our own environment. When you live in another country, the experiences become the fabric of your everyday life, only then do they become a part of your skin's memories. This is what the Peace Corps experience gives young people today. You enter the fabric of the peoples' lives in another country, so that their skin becomes yours, a bit of your skin is shared with them, and memories are stitched together. And when you come back to the United States, you no longer just belong to one country. You are more a part of the world.

. . . .

I am Nancy, the daughter of Paul and Frances Stone. My parents were Peace Corps volunteers. From its inception, my parents were supporters of the Peace Corps program, with strong beliefs that there were ways, beyond military to serve one's country. They wanted to be part of a program that fostered education and peace in the world. So in the 1970's, when my parents heard that the Peace Corps was taking families as volunteers, they decided to join.

There were many who questioned the wisdom of putting children in an environment where their health and education might be at risk. They feared that it might prove to be too much of a hardship and that the program would fail. However, my parents were willing to take that risk. The Philippines had the best program for my dad's skills, so my parents did their research; they spoke with Peace Corps representatives and assessed the situation in the Philippines, which was known to be a very corrupt country. President Marcos was strongly disliked, there was turmoil in the country, and young white children were known to have been kidnapped. Although, not my parents' first choice, it was the best job match, so with the support of family and friends, my parents made their decision. And that is how my three brothers and I ended up living in the Philippines for two years of our lives.

I am a mother myself now, with two girls ages 9 and 11. Sometimes, I sit back and reflect upon their childhood experiences so far, and wonder how I can give them some of the same experiences that I had growing up with my parents. Was it an important part of my childhood to live in the Philippines? Did it have an impact on my development and ultimately on who I am today as an adult? I know the answer, which is why I seek experiences for my girls that will stitch them into the world's fabric of skin.

The family with Peace Corps staff –
Project Director Jerry Nelson and Family Development Director
Jane Kargannilla

The Beginning of Something Big

PETER - 1971

I was just turning six in 1971 when my parents decided to go into Peace Corps for two years. It was to be their service to our country. Daddy was a farmer, even though we didn't have a farm. He said some day we would have a farm, but not right now. When he found out that Peace Corps was taking families as volunteers and that they needed farmers, he figured he could be a help in a poor country. Mommy was a preschool teacher, which meant she could also help in some way. The fact that they had four children didn't bother them in making their decision; they said it was a challenge for us and a good thing to do.

At the time my older brother, Daniel, was eleven, my sister Nancy was eight, and my younger brother, Matthew, was almost three. We were enthusiastic about joining Peace Corps, having of course no idea what it really meant or what the impact on us would be. Matthew and I didn't give it much thought, since at our age we were more centered on ourselves and being with our family, no matter where. We had no idea how long two years could be in a very poor country, living poor ourselves. Mommy and Daddy had some idea, however, and felt we were all up to it.

The first thing I remember about getting ready to move was that we had to give up our toys. We were told we wouldn't be able to take them with us. Mommy let us each take a couple of little toys, a few books, and pencils and paper, all of which we would have to carry in our backpacks. She also taped some of our favorite music for us because she believed bedtime music helped to settle us down. I know I really liked to listen to music before I fell asleep.

We were each allowed only two suitcases. It was comforting to learn that all of our toys, along with our furniture and household goods, would be put in storage for us until we came back and it was fun watching the movers box everything up and take it away in a big truck. I wanted to help but the movers didn't like that idea. I wonder what Mommy thought as she watched everything go, leaving us with only some clothes, some personal toilet articles, and Daddy's down pillow. Mommy and Daddy were told not to bring anything valuable—no watches or rings--because theft was a serious problem. And Mommy had to bring tampons, lots of them. At the time I didn't know exactly what they were, but there was this big deal about trying to bring a two-year supply, because tampons wouldn't be available where we were going. It was funny watching Mommy stuff the little boxes of tampons in the suitcases, but she managed. She couldn't have them sent to her because packages were often opened and some of their contents stolen, the mail to the Philippines was very slow, and some mail would never arrive at all.

Before we could leave, the FBI had to check out my parents and make sure they wouldn't pose a threat to our country or to the Philippines. They were even fingerprinted. We all had to get shots, including rabies shots, to keep us from getting all kinds of illnesses. The size of one shot depended on how big you were. Matthew got just a little needle stuck in him; mine was about the same size as his. Nancy's and Daniel's needles were a little bigger and Mommy's bigger again. But Daddy's was so big it looked like something he used to give shots to cows! There were a lot of shots, in our arms and in our rears. Some of the shots we would have to get again while we were in Peace Corps to make sure we stayed well. There was also this very big pink pill we had to take that tasted just awful. After looking at it I gave Mommy that "no way" look, so she crushed it up in a spoon and added some juice to it. It was still pretty awful tasting; but it went down faster that way. It was a real pain, I mean a real pain, all those shots and pills, but it was worth it because we didn't get any of the sicknesses the shots and pills were designed to prevent.

After all that we were finally in a plane, taking off from Dulles International Airport outside of Washington, D.C. and flying almost half way around the world. We landed at Dasmarinas, Cavite on Luzon Island in the Philippines, where on July 3, 1971 we began three months of training with the other volunteers, all of whom were involved with agriculture. We were called Group #43. The training was at the Union Theological Seminary, which had a farm. We were all—children and adults--considered trainees, and if we made it through training we would be placed on assignment on one of the many islands that made up the country.

The training period was sometimes hard on us, but Mommy quickly established a feeling of home, even so far away, and Mommy and Daddy's enthusiasm and humor, and the loving support they always gave us when things—like language, school, and the food — were difficult for us really helped. And we acquired a piglet as a pet, which helped us feel more at home. Daddy talked the man in charge of the pigs to let us have it. It was just a runt and was so small we had to put it in the oven for a few nights to keep it warm. We had a lot of fun with him. He loved to be washed and we liked feeding him with a bottle. The Filipinos found it amusing that we had a pig for a pet. They only kept pigs for food or to sell.

While we were in training we lived in a regular house, not much different from ours at home and we had a maid named Marietta who took care of Matthew when Mommy needed her too and of me too. Lots of time we got to go with Daddy when he was training on the farm. I really liked that.

The first morning at breakfast showed us how far we were from home. Breakfast was served cafeteria style, and there for us to think about eating were plates with pieces of cold fish—the heads, the bodies, and the tails were all served on separate plates. That didn't even tempt us. There were also cold greasy fried eggs, and to drink — evaporated milk with no water added! That was really awful. But we did our best. We added lots of sugar to the evaporated milk, I glared at the greasy eggs, made a face at the fish, and we all filled up on rice and bananas which, thank goodness, were always available. We didn't starve. The other trainees also had a hard time with the food, so after about a week the menu changed and there was more that we could think about eating. Breakfast was the biggest problem. They took away the cold fish and made sure the eggs were hot. The other meals were not so bad. And there was always rice and bananas.

The big issue for us kids was our schooling. Three-year-old Matthew didn't have to worry about school. Mommy did have to worry about getting rid of the pinworms he'd acquired. Daniel, Nancy and I were going to attend the school they had right on campus. They adjusted fairly well, even to wearing uniforms. They were enjoying making friends and learning about the culture. But me, I was another story. I was a very active child and I found it very hard adjusting to the hot weather and the school. School was a long day of sitting quietly with very little physical activity. One day while walking to school I decided to skip class and went instead to the building were Mommy and Daddy where struggling to learn Hiligaynon, the language of the area we would be going to. Daddy was doing okay, but Mommy was having a hard time. I added to their struggle by informing Mommy that I didn't like school and didn't want to go. And for three days I didn't. Obviously I was having some adjustment problems with more than just school. As an educator with an emphasis on child development, and as a parent who knew me very well, Mommy understood my unhappiness. She also knew it was important to get to the bottom of this because if I didn't adjust we might have to go home. Mommy talked with the teachers and decided that I would only go to school half day and would have more freedom to move around and to be with my parents or Marietta. I never adjusted to the heat.

It wasn't all hard those first three months; we did have fun. We especially enjoyed going with Daddy when he was learning how Filipino farmers worked. There were no tractors. Plows were made of wood; they looked like crooked sticks, each with a tiny blade on the end, and were pulled by cara-baos—a water buffalo. Corn was planted by hand, dropping the seeds into the row one by one. We all got to help plant the corn. Daniel got to help plow too. The rest of us also liked just playing around in the fields.

The Filipinos we met in training were quite taken with us as a family. This was the first time ever that Peace Corps Volunteers with children came to live and work with them, right where they lived and worked. The Filipinos were amazed that we were willing, as a family, to live the way they did and do without so much: we didn't even have a car.

While in training we were taken on many trips to learn about the country and see the way people lived, how they shopped and traveled. We were intro-duced to all the different types of public transportation and had to learn how to use it. We had never seen such poverty. We saw people begging for food or money, even children and women. We saw blind people, crippled people, people with hardly any clothes on, and people bathing beside the roads at water pumps. There were people everywhere and tons of children and none of them seemed to have very much.

Not all of the trainees made it through training. They couldn't adjust to the climate and the culture and had to go home. But Daddy and Mommy were successful. At the end of training there was a big party with lots of food and games. Mommy and Daddy and the others who had made it were sworn in as volunteers on October 2, 1971. We had a taste of what our life would be like for the next two years. We all felt ready for the challenge. I was even ready to try school in our new home.

We were all Peace Corps Volunteers, even Matthew. We each had a job to do. Daddy was going to work with farmers to help them improve what they fed their pigs. Mommy was going to work in preschools. The four of us? Our job was to be carriers of good will and friendship with Filipino kids. Mommy said she found great joy in seeing the ways we were all the same and different.

Soon after graduation, leaving our pig behind, we boarded a boat to go to the island of Negros Occidental to live in Bacolod City and begin our lives as Peace Corp Volunteers.

Paul learning to plow with a carabao

A rough boat ride to Bacolod City

Rough Seas and A Remarkable Hotel

FRANCES – FALL 1971

You have already met Peter, but before you meet the other three children who are sharing their story with you I need to fill you in a little bit on what happened once we became volunteers. When our training was over on the island of Luzon, Paul was assigned as an extension worker to the Bureau of Animal Industry, a division of the Department of Agriculture and Natural Resources, to work with pig farmers on the island of Negros Occidental. There we would live in Bacolod City. To get there we had to go to Manila, the capital of the Philippines, also on Luzon Island, stay overnight, and then take a boat to Bacolod City. Our stay in Manila was not much fun. It was raining and dreary and the slums, which are everywhere in Manila, looked sadder and poorer than usual. The water running off the streets and sidewalks was oily and dirty. Here and there drain pipes were plugged up, causing little flooded areas in and off the roads, making it hard to keep from walking in mud or getting splashed. To make things worse, while we were playing between rains in a park with a modern playground that seemed out of place in this poor country, Nancy fell and hurt her ankle. It quickly swelled up and turned black and blue. We took her to the hospital where an x-ray showed nothing broken, thank goodness. The doctor just wrapped it and told her to stay off it for four or five days and have it looked at it in Bacolod City. But it hurt a lot and ended our explorations of Manila.

We didn't get a very good night's sleep that night because the guest house where Peace Corps had arranged for us to stay was right in the middle of a noisy part of the city. We had to leave our windows open because it was muggy and hot, and we all had to share beds. We twisted and turned most of the night while all kinds of noises drifted up into our windows on the second floor. We were glad when morning finally came, but couldn't believe it when we were awakened at 6 a.m. to the strains of "White Christmas" drifting into our window. It was only October! We would soon learn that Christmas indeed started early in this country.

The Philippines are made up of 7,000 islands; our journey to Bacolod City was the first of many boat trips we would take. The boat we were on this time was not quite large enough to be called a ship. It carried both passengers and cargo, but the area for passengers was quite small. It was made up of a small first-class area, where there were individual cabins, and dorms, where most of the passengers slept. The dorms had rows and rows of double-decker beds, crammed in close together. There were also some bunks out on the upper decks, like sleeping on a porch or balcony. There was one dorm for women and children and one for men. Many of the small children slept on the beds with their mothers. It was pretty crowded. Peace Corps had booked us a first-class corner cabin below deck in the bow of the boat. It had portholes we could look out of, a double bed, two bunk beds, a couch, shower, sink, and toilet. We were very impressed. It was our first and last first class-trip. Aside from an older couple we didn't get to talk to, we were the only Americans on board.

We boarded the boat about two hours early and, after exploring a bit, watched it being loaded with a cargo that consisted of about anything you can think of– lots of plants, all kinds of food, long poles, small animals, and items so big they needed a crane. These included cars, trucks, a steam roller, an old rickety bus, and stones for some kind of masonry work.

The trip was to be more exciting than we had expected. We couldn't leave the harbor in Manila Bay because all the rain from the night before was the beginning of a typhoon that began pounding into the bay. (In the Pacific and in Asia a hurricane is called a typhoon.) We had to spend the night on the boat in the harbor with the boat rocking and rolling as the wind and rain whipped all around us. Dinner in the formal dining room was delicious, and included vegetables, a well-cooked, tasty fish, pork chops, a jello fruit salad, and of course rice. It was a much appreciated change after the meals we had had in training. But we ended up regretting that meal as we all got seasick before we even got back to our cabin. There we lay on our beds as the boat rolled around in the storm. It rolled over so far that one minute we could only see water covering the porthole and the next minute we saw only the cloudy stormy sky as it rolled back to the other side. It might have been fun if we hadn't felt so awful.

By the next morning Manila Bay had calmed down so we could start our trip, and our seasickness was forgotten. The kids were thrilled when we were invited to stand by the captain's wheel to watch the crew take the boat out of port. As we left the bay we noticed something interesting. Manila Bay is really polluted and the water is a dingy brown. Well ahead of us, where the bay entered the ocean, we could see what looked like a line drawn straight across the bay. This marked the edge of the pollution. We could actually see it. On one side of the line was the muddy, polluted bay and on the other the glistening clear blue ocean.

Once out of the bay the waves were still plenty big in the aftermath of the typhoon. Some bounced high onto the side of the boat, sending salty water and spray up and over the deck, to the delight of the kids. Except when we were in the open ocean between islands we followed the coastline from Manila to Bacolod City, the boat staying just far enough away from the islands to be in beautiful clear blue water; the terrible poverty mostly hidden from view. It was very deceiving. We spent the day relaxing on the boat and one more night with no seasickness. The next morning we docked in Bacolod City.

We didn't know where we would be living when we got to Bacolod City because Peace Corps left it up to us to find ourselves a house to rent. In the meantime, they put us up in the Sea Breeze Hotel, where it turned out we would be living for almost a month. The children thought it was absolutely splendid, and it was. From the outside it didn't look like much, but inside it was beautiful and air conditioned, obviously designed for a wealthy clientele. There were flowering plants and large foliage in large pots and little gardens everywhere. The lobby, dining room and lounge were all open to the outdoors with a view of the sea. We lived in only two rooms, but that didn't bother the kids because they had just about the entire hotel to roam around in, and there was a swimming pool. Roam around they did. The hotel became their home, our two rooms used mostly for sleeping, bathing, and wrestling with Paul on Sunday mornings before he got out of bed. After a few minutes of sharing in this fun I would make a hasty retreat.

The children had the run of the place. Peter and Matthew loved going up and down the curved, carpeted staircases, and Nancy and Daniel found their own special spots in the lobby and sitting areas where they liked to read. This happened because the owner of the hotel and his family fell in love with our family. While we found that Filipinos didn't always make friends easily with adults, they just opened their hearts up to children. Of course the kids took advantage of this and got to know not only the owner and his family, but the kitchen staff, waiters, cleaners, and everybody else who worked there as well. They were allowed everywhere, including the kitchen, the laundry room, and they even helped set tables in the formal dining room, with its white table-cloths, cloth napkins, little flowers in the center of the table, crystal glasses and china plates, where we ate along with the other guests. Most of the staff sort of claimed our kids as their own, and always knew where they were, even when I sometimes didn't.

This was the beginning of our life with Filipinos on a daily basis. It was not hard for the children to be respectful and considerate of all the different workers and their lifestyle, because they had been raised to respect the worth and dignity of all people. It was harder to adjust to some of the food. Take

Bird's Nest Soup, for instance, a much loved soup made from the nests (!) of little cliff-dwelling swallows. Places like hotels offered it as a delicacy. It cost a lot because it was not easy raiding the nests up on steep cliffs. Actually it was not bad after you got over where it came from and stopped thinking about the white stuff that was laced through it like a thin white ribbon. Another food that was different was *balut*, a food sold by street vendors everywhere you went. *Balut* is a hardboiled egg with a partly developed chick inside, complete with soft bones and the beginning of feathers. Filipinos thought it was delicious but admitted it was sometimes hard to eat so they often ate it in the dark. None of us ever got up the courage to try it; just thinking about what it was and watching others eat it was hard enough.

Our fancy hotel couldn't shield us from the extreme poverty that existed in this country. It was inescapable, along with the throngs of people that were everywhere. From our bedroom windows we had two views. One looked out to the pier where large boats came from Manila and other places, to beyond the bay to some distant islands, to beautiful sunsets. Our second view was very different. It was of raw black sewage moving sluggishly out of a huge pipe into a shallow inlet and eventually into the bay and the ocean. This included the sewage coming from our hotel. It was a smelly, ugly mess. In it we would often see men or young boys, standing knee-deep in the mess, digging for clams when the tide was low. When the tide was up we saw fishermen with their scoop-like nets walking through the waist-deep dirty water trying to catch shrimp. From what we could tell they didn't get much. On out a little farther in the filthy water we saw men in boats with fishing nets. This view was a constant reminder of the poverty of so many of the people. Seeing this day in and day out we began to understand why adults as well as little kids would steal food or clothes or whatever else they could get their hands on. And why the men dug for clams in the filth, even though it was against the law to be out there. We never saw anybody chase them away. What we never learned was whether what they caught was for food for a family or for sale or both. Either way, a real insight into a type of poverty we had never before imagined.

Daniel, Nancy and Peter started going to their private Catholic schools, as assigned by Peace Corps, a week after we got to Bacolod City. Private school was hard for Paul and me to accept at first, but we soon came to understand why public schools were not an option. After visiting several and seeing the poor classroom conditions, the hot dusty playgrounds with no equipment, the poorly clothed, sometimes sickly children, it was obvious that it would not be a healthy environment for our children. We also learned that any Filipinos who could come up with the money sent their children to private schools. The owner of the hotel sent his daughters, ages 10 and 17, to school in a limousine and insisted that our kids go along with them. This was not the way we lived in America; this was the way rich people lived in the Philippines. Each morning the chauffeur opened the door for them and off they went in air-conditioned splendor, as do most of the children of the wealthy. They returned home in the same manner. Some children took their nannies along to carry their books.

We had been told that while we were in the Philippines, although our work would be mainly with the poor, we would also be working and socializing with people from all walks of life. Well, we were really mixing with the upper classes right now, along with the staff. Nancy became friends with the owner's 10-year-old daughter. Maggie had a huge collection of Barbie dolls and many other toys. Nancy had never owned a Barbie doll. The owner also had toys for the boys – enough variety to keep all three joyfully occupied. I spent my time keeping up with Matthew, writing detailed letters home, and attempting to be a good listener as the children shared with me the ups and downs of their experiences in this new culture. It was not all fun and games by any means. It was not easy adjusting to everyday life, the food, the heat, and people staring at us, and the lack of our own car. Living in the city was also a challenge because we had always lived in a rural setting. I would wonder at times what I was doing here. But still, despite the many changes and differences and strangeness, I think we all did very well.

The whole family spent many hours roaming the city, getting used to public transportation, and getting to know the area we would be living and working in. Paul spent some time with the Bureau of Animal Industry, visiting some piggeries, and getting a feel for how the bureau was run and what exactly was expected of him. He took the children with him to piggeries a number of times, and they were always welcomed.

This was a very family-oriented society and most families had many children. Filipinos children were all over the place, at home, on the street, in the work-place, as much with their fathers as their mothers. I saw more dads helping care for their kids than I ever saw in the States. It was also very interesting to see that many families, even middle class and poor one, had nannies for their children. Nannies were called *yah-yahs*. Some wealthy families had a *yah-yah* for each child, and I was dumbfounded to find out in some families a *yah-yah* went to school to help the children with their work. Peter's school had a fence around it to keep the *yah-yahs* outside. There they sat and waited until it was time to take their charges home.

It took a while for us to find a house large enough for all of us that we could afford to rent, since Peace Corps salaries were pretty low. Finally, after a very long month, we found a house on the edge of the city. It was down a dusty, partly paved, partly dirt road that came to a dead end where a little gathering of the poorest of the poor called squatters attempted to make their homes. Our little neighborhood, like many in the cities and countryside, was a mixture: there were slums, a few middle-class dwellings, and some wealthy homes that were surrounded by fences and walls, with guards to keep out the poor. There were some open fields behind our house which we greatly appreciated. It was a good thing we left the Sea Breeze Hotel when we did or the kids would have been spoiled rotten.

The view out our bedroom window at the Sea Breeze Hotel

Delivering our furniture

Our Own Home,
Bacolod City

How exciting to be finally getting into our own home! Paul, Nancy, Daniel, and Peter cleaned and painted while Matthew and I packed up things at the hotel. We were ready! However things came to a halt on November 1, the day we had hoped to move, because it was All Saints Day. This is a big Filipino holiday when, businesses and schools are closed and people flock in large numbers to the cemeteries to pay their respect to the dead. Unlike what you might think, it is not a sad day at all, but rather a celebration of those who have died. It all starts the evening before, our Halloween, with a parade that includes Catholic priests, children, and some adults. Afterward, some people go to the cemeteries to keep an all-night vigil. The next day, November 1, people go to church, have family picnics, visit with each other, and the kids run about being kids. The day after that, All Souls Day is also a holiday but a much quieter one. So, we didn't move until November 3.

We were so happy to be moving in. We couldn't wait to see the new furniture Paul had ordered. The day it was to arrive we kept watching for the truck. Did I say truck? Not really! It was a rickety wagon pulled by three men, loaded way above their heads with our table, chairs, beds, and a bed to be used as our couch. It looked like a pile of poles and boards until it got up close and we could begin to tell that it was actually furniture. Because Paul couldn't find a bed for Matthew, he built him one with low

THROUGH THE EYES OF MY CHILDREN

sides. He had no power tools, no workshop, and no table to work on. He had to get down on the ground, just like a little kid, to hammer and saw. But he made a good bed.

We had brought no household things with us from the States and it was a challenge finding out where to buy them. It turned out that the open markets were where we could buy whatever we needed for the house and the family, as well as our food. These markets are sort of like our farmers' markets, but many are not as pleasant to shop in. While colorful and cheerful looking on the outside, with their bins of fresh food, clothing, household items, jewelry, wall hangings, and trinkets, the inside was often another story. Many were very large, dark, and dingy with dirt floors, poor lighting, and they were very hot and stuffy. Many only had leaky, makeshift roofs, so when it rained the markets became damp and the floors muddy. There were no bathrooms or places to wash your hands. Men, children, and sometimes women just stepped outside to relieve themselves. Within some of these markets the many smells of a poor society could make you reel, almost as if you'd been slapped in the face. It was within these markets that the majority of Filipinos, rich and poor, shopped – the wealthier ones sending their maids or errand boys. And this is where I shopped too. It was in the market, while buying cheap pink plastic dishes, that it fully hit me what I was going to have to do without for the next two years and, especially since we didn't have a car, how much time and energy would go into the almost daily grocery shopping.

I also bought some housekeeping items from a peddler who came down our street. He would walk along, loaded with colorful feather dusters, brooms, and other household utensils, his head peering out above the mass of his wares and his legs sticking out the bottom.

One thing the market didn't have was a supply of decent clothing. While we could buy basic underwear and very cheap t-shirts, dresses and pants were poorly made and in short supply. I hadn't been able to bring my sewing machine, nor could I afford to buy one, so I couldn't make clothes for us. And

I couldn't afford to shop in regular clothing stores. I didn't even know where they were. Caesar, our language instructor from training, who had become a very good friend, lived in Bacolod City and he told me I needed to go to a dressmaker or tailor to get most of our clothes made, just as he did. I didn't think I could afford that either, but it turned out to be the solution.

The dressmaker and tailor didn't use patterns. They just measured us, asked what style we wanted, helped us pick out the fabric, and sent us home. When we returned a week later, there were our clothes, well made, with a perfect fit. They even made the uniforms our children had to wear to school.

Our new home was small, just barely big enough for us, but it was ours and we were happy to settle in. It wasn't much of a house, but it had a nice backyard, which was important because of the hot climate and our love of animals. That space became a big part of our living area. We shared it with a pig, a dog, chickens, ducks, and uninvited snails of all sizes. The house had three bedrooms and one bathroom, which had a toilet and a cold water shower, with a drain in the floor. The kitchen, like most Filipino kitchens we saw, had a counter and a sink. I cooked on a two-burner stove that we had to buy. The one concession Peace Corps made to our having children was that we were allowed to have a refrigerator. That made life a little simpler.

There was also a garage, but without a car or lawn mower or much to store, that part of it wasn't very useful. But it also had a room for a live-in maid. At first I thought I might use it as an extra room but became convinced that as part of the Filipino culture, and to manage my life, I indeed needed a maid — a hard idea for me to accept. Caesar and his sister helped us find a maid. Once Delia moved in, it did not take me long to realize what a help she would be as I struggled with the increased household chores, taking care of the children, and working. She did know a little English, which was good because our Hiligaynon was pathetic. And her English improved faster than our Hiligaynon. Caesar visited us often and helped bridge the gap between Delia and us as we struggled to communicate.

The flimsy gate and smashed chicken wire fence around our house gave us neither security nor privacy. But the neighbors thought it was fine because they had an excellent view of our activities and weren't shy about watching us. We were the neighborhood novelty, live reality TV.

Finally we were all settled in and we began our daily lives as Peace Corps Volunteers. The kids continued going to their schools, but no longer in a fancy car with a chauffeur. Many times they were able to go with us to our work and learn about what we were doing. Had I not had Delia I wouldn't have been able to work, and work was a Peace Corps requirement. However, because of the children, they didn't expect me to work full time. Delia loved the children and was always home to watch out for them when I was working. Like many Filipinos, I often sent Delia food shopping so I could avoid the hassle of taking four kids and groceries on public transportation and coming home with my head spinning. And Delia enjoyed doing the marketing and was good at the bargaining that was part of doing business there.

Paul started his work for the Bureau of Animal Industry, learning about Filipino piggeries and figuring out how he might help the farmers improve the nutrition of their pigs. He began by visiting farms and talking to the farmers, hoping eventually to gain their trust and convince them that he had some workable ideas.

I found a part-time job as a teacher in the nursery school of the Department of Social Welfare in Bacolod City. My job was to help the staff improve their programs and teaching methods. I also got to work directly with the children, which was what I loved most. The challenge for both of us was to figure out how to blend our American ideas with Filipino practices, how to build bridges between our culture and theirs. We didn't want to change the way the Filipinos did things. Rather we wanted to show them how they could improve what they were doing using resources they had on hand. The secret was to figure out how what we knew could be used within the framework of their lives and culture. It was not our place to say, "This is the way we do it in the United States." Rather we would say, "Tell us how we can help you the most," or "How might this work for you?"

Another big challenge was to develop programs or methods that could continue after we left — to find and train Filipinos who could replace us. When we left we wanted to leave them something that could continue after we had gone, something that could work a little better for them. The weeks and months went by and we established ourselves as Peace Corps Volunteers within the Filipino culture and its overwhelming millions of very poor people.

The day of our leaving Bacolod City came sooner than we had expected. By the end of our first year as volunteers we knew that we would not be able to stay in Bacolod City and we moved to Baguio City, back on Luzon. But that story will unfold as Daniel, Nancy, Peter, and Matthew tell you about our life in two very different places in a very different culture.

Nancy and Matthew helping Delia with laundry

Meat booth at the food market

Slums in Manila

Stepping Into A Grand Adventure

DANIEL — 1971–1973

I was 11 when we went to the Philippines and turned 13 just a few months before we returned to the States. This was a very exciting period in my life, and I saw it as a grand adventure. There were so many different people, places, and things. I made many friends and found it easy to play and interact with the local kids. I had a few friends whose parents had lots of money and some who barely survived, they were so poor. The Philippines was a very poor country; slums were everywhere. There was no way to avoid them or the crowds of people that populated this country. No matter where we went there were lots of people and most of them were poor. I saw many homes in the city and country made of any scrap material that could be stuck together. I learned that these were usually the homes of squatters, people with no other place to live, who just set up camp wherever they could find an open space, forming their own little communities.

Many rich people's houses had walls built around them. Most of the walls were concrete and they often had broken pieces of glass or wire sticking out of the top to keep out the poor and hungry, some of whom would do anything to find food or something to sell to raise money. Some houses had armed guards, guard dogs, and even guard geese. We could hear the dogs bark and the geese honk when we walked by them. I knew that in the large cities there were neighborhoods of homes and shopping areas exclusively for the wealthy, but there were also terrible slums right next to many wealthy homes, as we saw just a short walk from our beautiful hotel in Bacolod City.

On the streets and in my little neighborhood, where rich, poor, middle-class, and squatters lived together, I saw children who were dirty, malnourished, hungry, and pot-bellied from worms staring at me with listless eyes. I watched kids who were hungry trap rats to eat. Beggars were everywhere – men, women and children. People clothed only in their underpants slept in the streets, covered only by a newspaper. There were naked little kids all over the place. This kind of poverty almost overwhelmed me at times. It made me think a lot about my own country and all that we had. I remember thinking that in our country there were animals that lived better than many of the Filipino people.

When we moved to the Philippines our lives changed greatly. So many things that we had taken for granted suddenly disappeared. No car. No stove with four burners. No oven. Where were the TV, washing machine, and bathtub? We did get to have a refrigerator, thank goodness. Volunteers without children were not so lucky. We had a toilet, but often we had to pour water into it to flush it. Drinking water out of the spigot? No way; it was polluted. Mommy had to boil all the water for drinking, brushing our teeth, and mixing powdered milk for us to drink. Fresh dairy products were a no-no because of possible unsanitary conditions. The powdered milk was pretty awful, but it was better than the evaporated milk we'd had to drink while we were in training.

Other foods were limited also; the risk of improper handling was too great. We were only able to have ice cream upon rare occasions, like at a hotel or restaurant that we knew for sure was safe. We couldn't eat corn, peanuts, or peanut butter because if they were not properly dried they could get a nasty mold on them that would make us very sick. How were we ever going to last for two years without our Sunday night popcorn, without peanut butter and honey sandwiches?

For two years, Mommy cooked all our food on a little two-burner gas stove that sat on the counter, and we bought our food in open markets. No more homemade cakes, pies, breads. She did try, once, to bake a cake in a pan over one of the burners. It was a total flop. However, she did become very good at cooking with only two pots: one for the rice that was usually cooked in the morning – enough to last the whole day, and one for the main meal, which usually consisted of vegetables, maybe some noodles, a little meat, and whatever spices we liked, cooked until well done. This was then served along with the rice. Our vegetables consisted mainly of green beans, carrots, onions, bean sprouts, and cabbage. Now and then we had potatoes and squash. Tomatoes were very expensive, so we didn't buy them very often. One unusual vegetable we used was called *sayote*. It was a light green on the outside, a little hairy, looked a little like a squash, and it was inexpensive. When you peeled it, it looked like a potato, but was very bland. We often used it in place of potatoes.

We all enjoyed the fresh fruits we could get like mango, papaya, melons, watermelon, pineapple, and *sarguelas*, this last a hard fruit with a big seed in the middle, about the size and color of a plum. It tasted a little bit like a plum, but was not as juicy. Mommy kept it on hand for snacks. In Baguio, a mountain area known for its plentiful vegetable gardens, lettuce, cucumbers, green peppers, and strawberries were added to our diet. Some of the fruits and vegetables were seasonal, except for bananas our standby. We ate lots of eggs; they were always available. In the market you bought eggs by the piece, picking out the ones you wanted.

The threat of disease was everywhere and Mommy was determined to keep us from getting sick. Every place we went we had to be careful about what we could and couldn't drink and eat. We had to soak our fresh fruits and vegetables, except bananas, for five minutes in water with bleach added to clean them and kill any dangerous bugs and the germs that could make us sick. We couldn't wade in creeks barefoot because of diseases, but almost all the water in creeks, rivers, or in roadside drainage ditches was so ugly and black and full of garbage that we didn't really want to anyway. The rice paddies did have clear water, but clear water didn't mean clean water and even here, when we helped plant rice, we had to wear boots because of a little snail that caused some terrible disease. Some of these illnesses could take months or years to get over. And some were fatal.

I must admit that all those dangers, along with the shots we had to get every six months, our yearly checkups that even included a sample of our "poop," and a series of rabies shots were overwhelming at first. I wondered those first few months if I would come out alive. One night during training, while I was lying in bed thinking about all this, a terrible thunderstorm came up. I could hear it from way off in the distance; it sounded like a huge horrible monster rolling towards me. As it came closer it got louder and louder and kept rolling and rolling. I could feel it rolling over our house. As lightning lit up the world, rain pounded on the house, and the monster seemed set to swallow me before it passed on by, I was sure I was a goner. If my parents had said "Let's go home," just then I would have shouted "Yes!" But they didn't. And I did, very happily, survive.

We had to pump water from a well by hand into our first home. It was quite a chore because we had to pump it into a little water tower from which it could then flow by gravity into the house. It was hard work, and it was pretty much up to Daddy to make sure it got done. If the water tower got empty, which it did on more than one occasion, we had to haul water by hand into the house.

Since it was always hot in Bacolod City, we did all our laundry outside and Mommy even let us bathe outside. The more we used water outside the longer the tank of water lasted for inside. That was Daddy's theory. We also collected water off the roof of our house into a huge barrel. We saved this in case we had a water shortage. Mommy washed her hair and shaved her legs with water from this barrel. A few times a woman from next door squatted by the fence and watched her do this, never saying a word. A couple of times she came into our yard and sat by the water pump while Mommy washed clothes and our pet duck happily flapped about in the water spilling over the laundry tub. Again she never said a word. Nor did Mommy, for they could not understand each other. Mommy just smiled and went about her work. Then she stopped coming; I guess the novelty of us finally wore off.

Running water was never a sure thing. Even when we lived in Baguio our second year in the Philippines, in a house that had running water inside, there were days when the public water system wasn't working and that meant no water. There were days when the water would run brown. Not good! Eventually Daddy got a trailer water tank from Peace Corps and had it filled, so we would have water when the public system wasn't working. All this added up to us being very careful how we used our water. And we could never drink it without boiling it first. Mommy soon learned many different ways to recycle water. She used water from doing the dishes to flush the toilet or water from doing the laundry to mop the floor, for instance.

We didn't use American money and had to adjust to pesos, which came in bills, like our dollars, and change that worked like our nickels and dimes. But the big thing about buying and selling was bargaining. Except for food, we rarely bought anything without bargaining. Often when a seller saw an American coming he asked for a higher price, because in his eyes Americans were tourists who had lots of money and didn't bargain. Here's how bargaining worked. You asked for a lower price than what you were told and the seller looked you in the eye and said no. You said your price again, and the seller named a price a little lower than his first price, but a little higher than the price you asked for, and back and forth you would go until the two of you finally agreed upon a price. The Filipinos were not use to seeing a family like us living like them with little money. They got a big kick out of bargaining with a *"Cano"* boy like me. (*"Cano"* was street slang for *"Americano"* – American.)

One of my first times at a beach I saw an old man with some shells I really wanted to buy. He was squatting in the sand with a basket of them. With encouragement from Daddy, I sat down in the sand in front of the basket and began to bargain. When the old man gave me a price, I got up my courage to ask for a lower one. He looked at me, shook his head, and repeated his price, so I repeated mine. To my surprise, he then offered a lower price, so I shook my head no and raised my price a little. Back and forth we went, until we finally came to an agreement. I got really good at bargaining; it was one of the many talents I brought home with me.

Mommy and Daddy didn't buy us very many toys while we were there because they couldn't afford them. I made my own slingshots, a big deal among boys there. The rubber ends of the slingshots were made from strips of old inner tubes, available in the public market. We used the slingshots for shooting at targets, mostly frogs and cans. With my friends I also learned how to make a bamboo cannon that made a lot of noise and smoke, which was the only point. We made volcanoes out of real mud and built little fires inside them. I even learned how to make a handmade gun that I never told my parents about. It didn't work very well, but it was fun to make. Another favorite activity was flying kites.

An exciting thing to do in Baguio was to find old tunnels that the Japanese had dug during World War II. My friends and I didn't try to go in them; we had been warned about the danger. We did dig in the dirt around the tunnels and found different types of shell casings. That was another thing I'm not sure my parents knew anything about. And there was nothing like putting firecrackers under tin cans to make a big boom and smoke. Firecrackers were readily available; heaven to a kid my age.

I also made myself a truck out of wood. I cut the wheels out of the spongy plastic from flip-flops, which everybody wore. Even the toy trucks in the market had wheels made from flip-flops. They used soda cans to make the springs and their trucks were brightly painted with designs. My truck wasn't as good as those in the market, but I had fun making it.

Recycling was important to the Filipinos. Anything and everything that could be used over and over was. Newspapers were used to wrap things you bought in the market and even for wrapping presents. Scraps of fabric were saved for making braided rugs. All types of cans and jars were saved and reused. The square five-gallon cans that held cooking oils were used by women to carry water and other items on their heads. Recycling would remain a part of our lives when we returned to the States.

There was one thing in the Philippines that we do not have much of in our country: public transportation. It went all over the country, not just in the cities. It was inexpensive and in some places it could take you from your front door to near anywhere you wanted to go. The jeepney was the main form of transportation all over the country. Jeepneys were World War II Army jeeps that had been left behind by the United States after the war and the Filipinos turned them into taxis. They had tops built over the backs and benches down each side. The side windows had no glass. Passengers entered through the open back. They were often painted in bright colors, with dangling beads and religious statues and pictures on the outside. Jeepneys set their own routes. You learned which ones went where and sometimes you had to take more than one to get near where you wanted to go. The driver would squeeze in as many people and their bags as he could. A full jeepney was a sight to see.

Then there were the buses. They ran all the time and went everywhere, within the town and throughout the country. And they were cheap. You'll find out more about buses in a later chapter.

In some cities they also used motorcycles with sidecars to transport people. One time we managed to get all six of us on a motorcycle. The driver wasn't supposed to put that many on, but Daddy talked him into it. Mommy and Daddy squeezed into the sidecar with Matthew, and Nancy, Peter, and

I were on the cycle with the driver. There were also the *calesas*, decorative two-wheeled carriages with roofs that were usually pulled by a skinny little horse. Again one time we gave it a try and Nancy got upset because the horse was so skinny and had a hard time pulling all of us.

There were very few cars since only the wealthy could afford them. A lot of people walked places and out in the farming areas you would see people riding in wooden carts being pulled by a carabao – water buffalo – usually with a person walking alongside it. Public transportation was likely to be a hair- raising adventure, especially in the buses, but you got to where you wanted to go. I rode all over the place in jeepneys in Bacolod City and the surrounding neighborhoods with my friends, and never had any kind of threatening experience

There is a great deal more my sister, brothers, and I can tell you, so turn the page and spend some time with us in the Philippines.

Daniel, friends, and his truck

The volcano Daniel made

Bus on a mountain road

Wild Rides

PAUL — 1971-1973

When you rode a bus in the Philippines you never knew what was going to happen. There were a few things you could always be sure of. The bus would be very crowded, with a combination of people and animals; it wouldn't be in a hurry; and there was a good chance it would break down along the way, since most of them were old clunkers that had seen their better days. We always joked that they were held together with rubber bands and bubblegum. But Filipino determination kept them going.

One day I was coming home from a piggery about an hour south of Bacolod City. I got on the bus and paid the conductor. All the buses had a conductor whose job was to collect money and help get the driver to stop when a passenger wanted to get off, which could be almost anywhere. He also had to keep peace among the passengers, especially the pigs and the fighting cocks. I was hot and tired and really wanted to get home, when all of a sudden a strange sound drifted up from the lower parts of the bus. We stopped short. Everyone woke up and my head wasn't the only one that hit the ceiling. The driver and conductor, together with a screwdriver, a wrench and, a piece of old inner tube, got out and disappeared under the bus. Many passengers got out too. Some headed for the bushes to relieve themselves; the rest stood around to watch. I was tired and decided to stay in my seat.

Since they had taken only a few tools with them, I figured that there couldn't be very much wrong. Probably the exhaust pipe was loose or something – a chicken maybe – was dragging on the ground. The chicken part wasn't too far-fetched because all available space was used for cargo storage. All sorts of boxes and trunks were tied onto the roof, sides, and back, and some were on the inside, right under your feet, all adding to the discomfort that I sometimes thought was the aim of buses. Lots of chickens and pigs were carried underneath, and with such a zoo anything could happen. The repair job was finished shortly and we were on our way. Two kilometers later we stopped again.

We stopped right in the middle of the road, as Filipino drivers almost always did. They hardly ever pulled off the road, even if there was room. The driver and conductor went through the same routine as before, and soon we could hear some tinkering down below. This time I couldn't resist having a look, even though I knew I would hit my head as I groped my way through the clutter and the people, most of whom stayed put this time. There didn't seem to be any buses that I could stand in and there were some in which Frances couldn't either. Anyway, with only one knock on the head I made my way outside. I couldn't believe what I saw. The driver and conductor were trying to figure out how put a broken universal joint back into operation with a piece of inner tube. Now a universal joint is a complicated mechanism that allows for bending in the drive shaft and is necessary for the forward movement of a vehicle. When it breaks you don't just stick it back in place, wrap it with a piece of inner-tube, and expect it to work. At least that is what I thought. But, they did just that, and the bus actually moved forward two more kilometers, when, lo and behold, it stopped again. Filipinos are not usually in any big hurry and it looked like this process was going to continue. So I decided it was time to ditch this bus and get another one. I was so close to home yet so far away. Fortunately buses came along very frequently and I didn't have to wait long for the next one. It got me to Bacolod City before it broke down and I caught a jeepney home. You may think that this was quite an adventure, but it was actually a pretty typical bus ride.

Then there was the time – Daniel was with me – when the bus got stuck on a bridge that was all muddy. It was one of those wooden bridges that had planks on the bridge for the bus wheels to follow, like railroad tracks. All of a sudden the wheels slipped off one of the planks and the bus started wobbling and tilting and felt like it was going to turn over. Everybody piled out of the bus onto the muddy bridge and walked off, while the driver, with his makeshift tools, somehow got it back on the planks and moving again. Daniel was really impressed.

Another time we were trying to get on a bus with so many others – all pushing and shoving – that we were worried we wouldn't make it. I told Daniel to go down to the back of the bus, climb in through a window, and save us some seats, as we had seen Filipinos do. Daniel pushed his way through the crowd, climbed up the side of the bus, squeezed through a window, and somehow managed to get and save us some seats on the wooden seat that went clear across the back. Eventually the rest of us pushed our way in and to the back, where we joined him. Without him, we would all have had to stand the whole way.

There were different types of buses in this country. Quite a few didn't have glass in their windows. Peter didn't care for these because when it rained everybody pulled wooden boards up to cover the windows, which made it dark, hot, and smelly. The darkness and heat bothered him.

Another kind of bus was completely open on the right side, with wooden benches going all the way across the bus to the left side that was closed in, one bench behind the other, with no center aisle. You had to climb onto the bench and slide down it to your seat. Nancy thought those were really scary, especially on those narrow mountain roads, where it looked like the bus was going to fall right off the road down the mountain. It was in Baguio, on the mountain, that we had our first experience with the one-sided bus.

There were of course the tourist buses that we never did get to use and some they called express that were a step up from the rickety ones we rode.

As a family we didn't have to use the buses a whole lot; just when we went on long trips out of Bacolod City or Baguio. Most of the time we rode the jeepneys, and we were fine with that.

Daniel helping change a tire

A fancy jeepney in Bacolod City

The Same But Different

NANCY - 1971-1973

I was 8 and 9 years old when we lived in the Philippines. Moving to and living in another country was not something new for me. My family had lived for almost a year on a tiny, very poor island called Virgin Gorda in the British Virgin Islands in 1970. At the time Daddy and Mommy worked for the Farm & Wilderness Camps in Plymouth, Vermont. They were sent to the island to start a farm and camp for the local and stateside children. On that island 95 percent of the people were black and my brother Daniel and I went to the all-black elementary school. There was only one other white boy. Peter and Matthew were not in school yet. The only white people on the island were some hotel owners, two preachers, and the few tourists. We didn't know them and saw very little of them.

Our neighbors and friends were very poor. Their homes were small and for the most part made out wood with galvanized metal roofs, and windows without glass or screens. Many people had to go to a public well for water and caught water off their roofs. Some cooked outside. Some didn't have electricity. I liked living on the island because the people were very friendly and made me feel very much at home. I also liked being outdoors, in the country, and so near the ocean. Living on Virgin Gorda helped to prepare me for the Philippines and how we would live there.

While parts of my life would be different from my life in the United States, much of it would be the same as that of any girl my age living on a farm in rural America. I was used to being in the country, being around animals, and helping on a farm, even though we didn't yet have our own farm. When I was in the Philippines, even though I was immersed in a different culture, I didn't really think of my life as being different. The Filipino culture became my own and within it I continued to act my age and to be me. I just did it Filipino style with Filipino kids: it was the same but different.

There were some things in the Philippines that made it a little hard to live within the culture. During our first year, when we lived in Bacolod City, we lived among people who didn't know or see many white folks. They, especially the mothers, were fascinated with our white skin and constantly pinched our cheeks. This was a display of affection, according to our Filipino friends. Perhaps, but I still didn't like it. They also liked to touch our hair, especially Peter's and Matthew's, because theirs was very blond. People stared at us constantly and watched us for two reasons, according to Mommy: Filipinos really loved kids; and they couldn't get used to an American family who lived among them. Remember, this was the first time Peace Corps had whole families as volunteers. Until now there had only been single volunteers. It took a long time to get used to pinched cheeks and being stared at so much. I'm not sure we ever did.

Some of the food was very different and while some was okay there was some that was just gross, as far as we were concerned. One day we all went to visit some people who had a big pot out in their dirt yard, boiling something that looked very strange. I kept trying to figure out what it could be. It looked like fire hoses rolling around in bubbly dirty brown water. Daddy told me they were carabao intestines. He then went into what we call his educational mode and explained how Filipinos used all the parts of the animal that they possibly could so as not to waste any. Fine, I thought, as long as I didn't have to eat intestines.

Daddy had us try some dog meat when we were visiting another family. The meat was dark and looked like little pieces of fried meat, so we didn't think anything about it. He didn't tell us it was dog meat until after we had eaten some. Good thing. He asked us what it tasted like and I told him that it didn't seem to have any particular flavor and that he better not do that again. One time we went to a pig roast and I ate a pig's tail. It was deliciously crunchy. Another time we went to a pig roast and I saw them kill the pig before roasting it. They didn't cut off the head. They just stuck a big stick through its mouth and out its rear end and put it over the fire. I didn't eat any pig that night.

There was lots of food I did enjoy, especially the many different types of fruit. Particularly good was the *kalamansi*, a small green lime-like fruit that was used like lemons. It made a drink that tasted even better than lemonade and didn't taste like limeade either. Mommy made it all the time for us. Because we had a refrigerator we could have it cold rather than room temperature and that made it so much more refreshing. I also liked fried rice, a very common way to use cold rice at the end of the day. Mommy would add scrambled eggs to it along with a little shrimp. That was the most common way it was done everywhere. However because it was expensive, we didn't use much shrimp. Some people add green peppers, but Mommy didn't very often because we didn't like it that way. Coconuts were readily available in Bacolod City and were often served as a treat in many of the homes we visited. The coconut was split in half and the sweet milk inside was saved to drink. And the chunks of fresh coconut tasted so good!

Of course, like children almost everywhere, I went to school. Once we moved into our own home in Bacolod City we rode a jeepney to and from school, along with some other kids. It came to our neighborhood every day to pick us up. I didn't like the first school I went to. It was OK in the beginning. I was not bothered by being the only white child in an all-girls Catholic school taught by nuns, and since they taught in English, I didn't have a language problem. What was hard the first few days was eating lunch by myself, until I started making friends. But I stopped liking the school because it was very strict and I had to wear a uniform every day: a navy blue skirt and white blouse, just like everybody else, from first grade through high school. One day my teacher got mad because Mommy had put a pink ribbon in my hair and clipped a little pin to my blouse. She told me my ribbon had to be brown or black and that I couldn't wear a pin. One day I didn't spell a word correctly and the teacher made me stand in the corner. It was very embarrassing and really upset me. One day I failed a test and the teacher announced it to all the class. I wanted to sink down in my seat and hide. And one day I didn't do well on an assignment and it was grabbed by one of the kids and passed around the class. It was all I could do not to cry. I was a good student and I had always enjoyed school and I was proud of myself and my accomplishments. That school didn't make me feel proud at all and I was beginning to dislike it very much. When Mommy saw a photo of me at school she almost cried because I looked so unhappy, and she now understood why I had been out of sorts at home, not like my usual happy self. I hadn't told my parents how unhappy I was, which was probably dumb. After the Christmas holidays my parents took me out of there; thank goodness!

One of the things I did like at school, at first, was learning how to embroider. I learned several different stitches and had to sew sets of each stitch in straight lines across a piece of cloth. Row after row I made those stitches and I got bored, bored, bored and I began to dislike doing them. As soon as I was out of that school, I cut away the rows of stitches and started over, making my own design. That was a lot more fun, it looked really pretty, and there was nobody to scold me. Mommy tutored me the remaining few months of the school year. When we moved to Baguio – in the mountains and much cooler – I went to a school I really loved.

My second school, a missionary school, was called Chefoo School. We lived close enough to it so that Peter and I could walk. Slowly we wandered on our way, on and off the path, up the hill, past the little group of squatters' huts all huddled together, to our school's pretty white buildings. We rarely saw any of the squatters themselves and I often wondered what they did when it rained, how they stayed dry or warm.

My teacher at Chefoo, Mrs. Edwards, was from Canada. She gave me a pretty pink Bible. Peter's teacher was from Australia and he enjoyed being a first grader with her. He had more freedom to move around and play than he had had at his school in Bacolod City, and he loved science, art, and making things out of clay. Like me he had had a hard time in his first school because it was so strict. At one point a teacher had smacked his hand with a ruler.

It was so different at Chefoo and so much fun. My classmates were from a lot of different countries. I loved getting to know the teachers and kids from so many places. On cool days we sat around the fireplace and listened to stories, and we often sat around the piano when singing songs. Once again I could color a picture any way I liked. Not like at the other school, where the sky always had to be blue, the grass green, the sun yellow, and everything else exactly the way the teacher wanted it. We put on a play and I was a tree. I fell down, but the teacher didn't embarrass me when that happened, so it was okay. It was there that I learned my multiplication tables. I had fallen behind in math and reading in Bacolod City, but I quickly caught up and that gave me a delicious feeling of accomplishment, especially since I loved to read and write stories.

The majority of Filipinos were poor, many extremely poor. This meant that many of them would steal anything they could get their hands on, often to sell for food and other necessities. Mommy and Daddy accepted it as a part of life in the Philippines we would have to adjust to, since they had been told it was a very big problem all over the country. We had things stolen in Bacolod City and in Baguio. For instance, Mommy had been told never leave her laundry out on the line overnight. She left it out overnight all the time in the United States, but here, she was assured, it would be stolen. One time she left a sweater hanging out up against the house and went on an errand. When she got back, the sweater was gone. Daniel's bike was stolen during the day right under Mommy's nose. One minute it was leaning against the house, then it was gone and we never saw it again.

It wasn't just Americans who had to guard against theft. One day our friend Caesar had six pairs of his good pants stolen, during the day, right off the clothesline up against his house, while his sister was inside. It was hard always to remember to take the precautions necessary to keep things safe. Dealing with theft and loss was one of the most difficult things to adjust to in our life in the Philippines, but Mommy and Daddy helped us to understand and accept this in a way that did not prejudice us against poor Filipinos.

I had taken piano lessons while in the States and even though we couldn't afford a piano I was able to take them while we lived in Bacolod City because I became friends with Julie and June Sarmiento. They lived across the street and invited me to practice on their piano and have lessons with their teacher. Daniel became friends with their brother Andre. The Sarmientos lived in a mansion with a low wall around it, and a fence on top of the wall. It also had lots of plants inside the wall making it hard to see into the yard. Our house looked sad and small compared to it and it was completely different from the homes of some of the other kids I knew in the neighborhood, which were made of wood and metal scraps. In the Philippines there were some very rich people and millions of very poor people. There were not very many like Caesar who was middle class — not poor, but also not rich. I guess we were like Caesar. Most Americans would have seen us as poor, however, because of the things we didn't have, like a stove, TV, car, washing machine, record player, and because we lived in a small shabby house. Mommy and Daddy would talk with us about these differences to help us understand this very different place we lived. It was not easy to see all these poor people when there were some people who had so much. As for us, we were just fine.

After we finished our training and moved to Bacolod City, Mommy and Daddy got one of their first lessons in living the way people did in this country. The lesson was this: in the Philippines everybody, even many poor people, had a maid. It was funny, because while Mommy resisted it, the Filipinos she met couldn't understand why she didn't have a maid, a laundry woman, a yard person, and a *yah-yah* for each one of her children. They didn't understand why Mommy, and not a *yah-yah*, would walk with me to a birthday party. She always had to explain that in America she couldn't afford a maid, much less a *yah-yah*. I don't think they believed her.

We children thought that having a maid would be really neat. We had never had one before and now, we thought, we wouldn't have to help with the housework. Wrong! Mommy was not going to let having a maid excuse us from the responsibility of helping to care for our home. So we did help with the housework, as we had always done. When we lived in Bacolod City, I helped Mommy and Delia wash clothes in a big tub at the water pump in our backyard. We used cold water and rubbed the clothes up and down on a scrub board. We had a lot of clothes to wash, being a family of six. Mommy had to also wash our sheets and towels by hand. Since we didn't have a clothes dryer, we had to hang them all on a clothesline. I think doing all that laundry helped Mommy understand why she needed a maid. We didn't have non-wax floors or carpets either, so that meant the wooden floor had to be waxed and polished. Months would go by between waxing, but polishing was done every day with a coconut husk. Delia, our maid, taught us how to do it, and we all helped. She gave us a coconut husk cut in half and told us to put one foot on the husk, and then she gave us this little broom. We were to slide the husk back and forth and round and round over the floor, sweeping up the bits of husk that were ground off in the process. The Filipinos could really make a shiny floor with that husk. It was fun, but hard work. We would use a husk until it wore down to almost nothing and then buy a new one at the market.

In the Philippines, as at home, and like many children all over the world, I felt the sweet build-up of anticipation the day before my birthday, and Christmas still seemed to take a long time to come. I loved jumping into a pool of ice-cold water on a hot summer day. I cried, like any child, when a pet died or was stolen. I had the same feelings there as at home of warmth and security when my parents tucked me into bed at night. All those things were still a part of my life in the Philippines. As a child in a Peace Corps Volunteer family I came to the realization that I had a perfectly ordinary childhood in an extraordinary place. I grew up different, yet the same as many children all over the world.

Nancy makes a new friend

Nancy's birthday with friends

Fleeting Images

MATTHEW – LOOKING BACK

Not long ago my mom asked me what I remember about being in Peace Corps.
I looked at her in a rather blank sort of way. What did I remember? Well, to
begin with I was only turning three years old when we went into Peace Corps
and just turning five when we returned to the States. So to tell you the truth,
I don't really remember much of anything. While we were in the Philippines
I even forgot that I had lived in the United States and what it was like there.
I don't think very many people remember much of anything between birth
and five years. What they do remember are really big things like this: one
day when I was four I was running down a road with Peter and Nancy and
suddenly slipped and fell in some gravel. I cut my upper lip very badly, lots of
blood, lots of crying. That is all I remember. Peter remembers more details.
He said that I had fifteen stitches and that it was a "nice mess." Not surpris-
ingly, my mom remembers a whole lot more about that day: getting me to the
hospital, sitting with me, and holding my hand while the doctor stitched me
up, and me crying, even though my mouth had been numbed and it didn't
hurt. But all I have is a fleeting image.

Most of the things I remember about that period of my life are like that,
fleeting images, flashes of light racing across my brain, carrying a piece of an
event with no details, no beginning or ends. It's like looking at a photograph
that shows only a little part of a story

Here are some more:

– As I watch Delia polish the floor with coconut husks, I hear the big German shepherd around the corner barking. Nancy, Daniel, and Peter were running past him on the way home from school. Peter says he remembers having to pass that dog daily. I just have this snapshot.

– I am washing clothes in Mommy's old wringer washing machine with Vicky, who was living with us in Baguio. I put the clothes in the wringer and Peter grabs them as they come out, pressed very flat. But then I don't let go soon enough and my left arm is in the wringer too, right up to my shoulder. My mother remembers taking me to the doctor, that I had to keep my arm in a sling for a week, and that my arm turned black and blue. To show how small I was, the sling was made from Daddy's large red handkerchief. She remembers that I really liked the sling and, when I went to school with her, her students did too.

– My family calls the little mountain behind our house in Baguio Matthew's Mountain because I like to climb it with them. Halfway up is a long thick rope that I love to grab hold of and get pushed up into the air, shouting with joy. At the top of the hill is a ditch the size of the Grand Canyon (to my four-year-old eyes) that dares me to cross. I run and hop across the narrow board bridging the gap, ending up safely on the other side.

Does that memory come from having seen over and over the movie of our family climbing Matthew's Mountain? Or do I remember the event? Because of the movie, I know it happened in the Philippines, but that type of thing could also have happened in the States.

– I reach the sky by bouncing up and down on my 2x6 board propped up on a white five gallon pail. Most of our toys were simple and homemade.

– I cling to my mother as yet another Filipino reaches out to pinch my cheek. They are always pinching my cheek and I don't like it.

–Wham! Dad's borrowed truck "kisses" the rear end of another. I don't remember anymore about it.

Since we didn't have a car, we all remember the truck because borrowing it from the nuns my mother worked for when we lived in Baguio was a big deal. I don't remember that it was a tinny little blue truck with seats down the sides like a jeepney. It was called a Ford Fiera according to Daniel. Everyone said the cab was so small that Daddy could hardly fit into it. Peter said Daddy looked like he was packed into a tiny little box, he was so squished up. He had to bend his head way over to look out. Everybody else thought the truck looked like an overgrown matchbox truck. But all that I don't remember.

– I am up on a high diving board with my dad. He holds me in his arms and I am scared as I look down at the water. He jumps off the diving board and down, down, into the water we go. I want to do it again.

– I ride in a blue jeepney to school.

– I eat lots of bananas and lots of rice.

As you can see my memories really are just snapshots. They are a lot of little pieces of a very big and important part of my life. Since I remember so little, people often ask if it was worth having me spend two years in another country as a Peace Corps Volunteer at such a young age. According to my mother, it was important because while I don't remember much, the experience had an impact on me in ways I didn't realize then but would become an important part of how I developed as an adult. Is she right? Did the experience have an impact on me? Well I still love bananas, I don't eat a whole lot of rice, I still don't like to be pinched on the cheek, and I definitely find my life enhanced by people of different cultures, races, and religions. Peace Corps played a part in helping me develop an appreciation of the differences among people, and the worth and dignity of all individuals.

As you read the story of my family's experience in the Philippines you will find me in it many times. Since I do not remember many events or have only snapshots of memories, my mother will tell my part of the story for me, and you will find out more about what my life was like as a very young, very blonde, little white boy among people who were all brown with straight black hair. For two years I don't remember seeing any white children other than my sister and brothers. As a matter of fact, I didn't think much about the different skin color. It was just a fact of life. That most of the people I knew were very poor didn't mean anything to me either. I played with other kids and stayed close to my family, just as any three-to five-year-old would do whether in the Philippines or the United States or anywhere else.

The jeepney Matthew rode to school

A typical roadside stop in the mountains outside of Baguio

A friendly pig watching us

Pigs and Kids In Bacolod City

DANIEL – 1971

Believe it or not, Nancy, Peter, even Matthew, and I really were considered to be Peace Corps Volunteers and that meant that we also had a job to do. Compared to our parents' work, ours was pretty easy. We were supposed to help spread good will. It sounds simple, but it wasn't always so easy, especially in the schools and in the way kids did things together. For instance some of the kids in the neighborhood would throw rocks at us, then laugh and run away. We never did figure out why they did that. Maybe they saw us as different and strange, which made them a little scared of us. Maybe they envied us the things we had that they didn't. Luckily we were able to overcome these hurdles, pretty much by just ignoring them and talking with our parents. We didn't let this kind of thing get in the way of doing our job. What we had to do was go to school, play, help our parents and others, make friends, and just plain have fun. It was pretty easy to have fun and not all that hard to make friends.

Actually the four of us definitely helped our parents break down cultural barriers, because many of the poor Filipinos Mommy and Daddy worked with were unsure about American adults. But when they saw the four us with our parents, they often became more welcoming. They thought our father was a really macho man because he had four children. Having us around may have made Daddy's job a little easier, because we sometimes got to be with our father when he was working on farms. The farmhands were always very friendly to us, and we never felt we were in the way. One of the reasons we were able to go with our parents was that there were many holidays and school vacations. In the States we had snow days. In this country you had rain days.

Daddy's job was to help farmers to improve the feed they gave their pigs. He found out that molasses, a by-product from making sugar from sugar cane, was being dumped into rivers by many of the sugar centrals, where sugar was made. He ran some experiments, adding molasses to the ration that made up the pig feed the farmers bought, because it was clear that one of the things missing in the feed was sufficient energy. Molasses was the perfect remedy for this since it was easily available. He was able to show the farmers that adding molasses increased the energy level of the feed – and also added a few minerals and vitamins. Some of the wealthier farmers were skeptical, but others were more open and could afford to buy the fortified feed. But the most important part of Daddy's work was to convince the poorer farmers that this was a good thing, and to figure out a way to sell the feed with molasses at a price they could afford. Most of them fed their few pigs whatever was available for free, such as garbage, rice hulls, and banana leaves. Daddy was able to convince a farm co-op to make the feed at a price affordable to the farmers. He also wrote a little booklet explaining how to make the feed properly and how to train workers to actually do it. The right amount of molasses was very important. Daddy found out the best ration mix was 70% grains with 30% molasses. This made a gooey, sticky, lumpy, high-energy feed that the pigs loved.

When we moved to Baguio City after nine months, Daddy left behind people he had trained and the co-op was willing to carry on the program, but he never found out if it continued or not. For all kinds of reasons, from finances to new people on the job to lack of sustained interest, without his presence it could easily have fallen apart. This is a good example of the type of thing that Peace Corps Volunteers tried to accomplish to help improve things for the people they worked with.

It was always fun to go with Daddy to the piggeries. Pigs there were just like pigs at home. Some were friendly and would stand up with their front legs on the boards of their pen to greet us. We could scratch their ears and rub their heads. We especially loved the piglets and loved watching them nurse. When the mother lay down on her side, the piglets came running and started rooting around at her tummy until they grabbed hold of a nipple and began to suck milk. They made happy little grunting noises as they nursed. Every now and then two of them would fight over a nipple, squealing and nipping at each other until one finally got a hold and hung on until the other one gave up. Some of the piglets were big enough to grab hold of a nipple while the mother was standing. They sat on their little rear ends and sucked and sucked until she walked away. Then they would squeal and run after her. The piglets were very playful, even when they weren't nursing. They ran around squealing and bumping into and nipping each other, and then they would all pile up together and go to sleep.

At the big piggeries, the pigs were housed in barns with one side open so they could go outside. Some of the farms were very clean and the pigs had clean water in the barns to lie in to stay cool. Some only had mud outside but that was okay with the pigs. A happy pig was one that had water or mud to sleep in when it was hot. We saw pigs of different sizes in pen after pen sleeping all stacked up in a big pile and watched as one came to join the group. With his nose he rooted his way in among them and plopped down into the pile, paying little attention to the disruption he caused, as the others grumbled and moved about to make room.

We also saw the farmers giving the piglets shots. The piglets didn't like it at all because the farmer held them upside down by their hind legs causing them to squeal really loudly, but then they would quiet down. Maybe all that blood rushing to their heads quieted them. We don't know. We do know we always had a great time visiting the piggeries.

Daddy also spent time going with farmers to see beef cattle and milk cows. I got to go with him on one of his overnight trips. We actually went on a small plane to get to the farm. It was interesting seeing those hot dusty farms and seeing how the farmers worked with their cattle. Those trips could be really exciting, and Daddy will tell you about one in the next essay.

While Daddy was working with piggeries, Mommy was working with little kids and teachers at a daycare center in Bacolod City. Sometimes we got to go with her too, but not so often. Matthew liked to go with her, but the rest of us liked going with Daddy, because there was more to see and do. Mommy worked more with the teachers than she did with the children, helping them develop different ways of doing activities and introducing new ones. It was not easy, because supplies were not easily available and things didn't always work out the way she'd thought or hoped they would. Her experience trying to make play dough is a good example of this.

It seemed like such a good idea. The community center couldn't afford to buy play dough and it was easy and inexpensive to make. But after she told the teachers what ingredients she would need, it dawned on her that if she used flour for play dough there would be less for the hungry families who got supplies of it from the center. The teacher told her that that was not a problem because they had flour from the United States in bags they couldn't use, because they had bugs in them. Why were there bugs in that flour? Mommy suspected it had to do with the age of the flour and the lack of good storage. As far as the teachers were concerned, Mommy could use all the flour she wanted. Imagine her surprise when she opened up a bag and thousands of mealy worms came crawling out. She was literally speechless, and her great idea faded away. Such was the life of a volunteer.

The teachers also complained that the powdered milk they got from the United States was not good either; it was lumpy and hard and tasted awful when mixed with water. And of course, if it was mixed with bad water, it made the children sick. Once mixed, it had to be refrigerated, and most of the families didn't have either good water or refrigerators. Mommy knew exactly what they meant about it being hard to mix because she had used government powdered milk. So despite good intentions; a lot of flour and powdered milk went to waste or was thrown to the pigs. Mommy was glad that the pigs got some of it, but to her the hard lumpy powdered milk and buggy flour were examples of our country trying to do good without adequately assessing what would or wouldn't work.

Mommy became good friends with Terry, one of the teachers, and visited Terry in her home out in a *barrio*, a Filipino village. One time Nancy went with Mommy because Terry had a new baby and wanted Nancy to see it. Nancy will tell you about the trip.

"It was always exciting for me when I got to go some place with Mommy without my brothers. This morning was going to be really special because we were going to get to go inside a real nipa hut, which I had wanted to do. Actually, I thought it would be really neat to live in one. All the nipa huts in the *barrio* were on stilts about six feet off the ground for protection from flooding because the land was so flat. This was not wasted space because it was often where animals were fed and rested, children played, and some chores were done. The huts were made out of bamboo, with thatched roofs made from the leaves of nipa palms. The floors were made of wide bamboo strips that were close together, but because they were uneven you could see through them down to the ground. Still, the floor was strong enough to hold the family, even with visitors. Sweeping was easy; the dirt just went right down through the cracks. The few windows had no screens or glass, and when it rained they had shutters to let down. Nipa huts were cooler than houses like ours in Bacolod City, which had a hot metal roof.

"We were going to see Terry's four-week-old baby and to have lunch with Terry and her family. The fact we had been invited showed how much Terry liked Mommy and was comfortable with her. Terry knew that Mommy wouldn't make her feel ashamed of her home. That was a really big deal because many

Filipinos were always concerned about being made to feel ashamed of what they were doing, or what they did or didn't have, even among themselves. So it really was an honor. And then I found out Terry had named the baby after her: his middle name was Francis. I couldn't help but feel a little proud.

"Terry's home was in a *barrio* out in the country. There was lots of shade and it felt a little cooler than in town. There weren't any lawns here. The land was all dirt, with the usual pot-bellied, multi-colored skinny pigs, skinny dogs, chickens, and children wandering around. There were old people sitting about too and probably some of them were watching over the kids. We found Terry's home and climbed the ladder up into it. The hut had four rooms and a kitchen that was half a room, or maybe more like a big bay window sticking out of the hut along part of a wall. I could hardly believe it when I saw how many people were living there: Terry, her husband, their four kids, a grandfather, and Terry's sister and brother. I counted nine people. There was no bathroom. There was a privy a little way off from the house, and I really don't know where they bathed. They had to haul water into their home, and they cooked over an open fire in the kitchen. They had very little furniture, and I wondered where everybody slept or if they even had beds. I didn't see any. Even I could tell that Terry and her family were really poor.

"While Terry visited with Mommy and me and nursed her baby, the grandfather and Terry's brother cooked the meal and her sister took care of Terry's one-year-old baby. Everybody pitched in to help. Lunch was simple, with plenty of rice as usual. We also had some fish, bananas, and fresh coconut that was still in its shell. To drink, we had the always favorite orange soda pop. I got to hold the baby. He was so tiny; it was hard to believe that I was once that small.

"Terry's family depended very much on her job at the community center, where she worked with Mommy. But she was not going to be able to return right away, because the center couldn't afford to take her back for two or three months. Even though her baby was so young and she had three other small children, she wanted to go back to work as soon as possible. Luckily she had family members with her who would take care of her kids while she worked. But it would probably be the grandfather who would be the most responsible for them. Terry didn't tell us what her husband did, or if he even had a job. I had no idea what the family would do while Terry couldn't work. She told Mommy that she wished she could get a sewing machine, because that would help her family, but she couldn't afford one. We had a good time there, but it made me realize how lucky I was and that as much as I'd thought I wanted to, our family really couldn't live in a *barrio* in a nipa hut."

Paul and a farmer discussing the importance of greenery in a pig's diet

The road makes a good place to dry rice.

Cattle Drive

PAUL – FALL 1971

I spent my time doing two things my first two months as a Peace Corps Volunteer. The first was visiting the many piggeries on the outskirts of the city. I visited some with my boss, Dr. Florento Romero, and two co-workers I had been assigned to work with as a Livestock Extension Worker. Others I visited on my own, traveling on my little motor scooter that took me through the dusty hot streets at a fairly good little clip. I visited the piggeries of very wealthy farmers that raised up to a couple hundred pigs all the way down to the little backyard piggeries of farmers who were barely scratching out a living, with one or two skinny sows and their piglets. The backyard farmers raised the pigs to sell, not eat, to raise money for special occasions such as graduations, weddings, funerals, and even school expenses. These were the farmers I wanted to work with and I was not pleased when I found out that most of my work was going to be with the wealthier ones.

The second thing I did was spend hour upon hour sitting and waiting for my boss or my co-workers to finally start the day. Once they did start they were in no hurry to get anything done. I was to find this to be the case with most of the Filipinos I worked with. As an American and as a farmer, I was used to making things happen, and on time. This just was not the case in Filipino culture. It was one of the hardest things to adjust to in being a Peace Corps Volunteer, but I did my best.

One day Dr. Romero wanted me to go with him to help him with a special government program. We were to go up into the mountains in the southern part of Negros Occidental to round up 40 beef heifers that were going to be dispensed to farmers in that area. Once a heifer had calved a few times, the farmer would have to give a heifer calf back to the government to give to another farmer to continue the program. I was told to be ready at three o'clock in the morning and that we would be staying overnight. I was up and ready, only to wait for more than an hour for Dr. Romero to show up. Then we went to wake up the driver of the truck. We were now two hours late leaving Bacolod City.

I groaned as I squeezed into the cab of the truck and saw the hard wooden seat I was going to have to sit on. I was glad to see a thin little cushion on the seat, better it than no cushion at all. There wasn't any cushion on the wooden ceiling though, and at six feet tall, I knew what would happen every time we hit a pothole or a bump. After a jeepney with some fellow workers joined up to follow us, we finally got on our way.

Progress was slow but steady as we traveled south along the coast on a fairly good, partially-paved road. We kept stopping for coffee and warm soda pop – no drinking water, going around rice that was drying on the paved sections of the road, and dodging occasional pigs and chickens. And we slowed way down when we got behind a cart being pulled by a carabao. The trip to the turnoff into the mountains, which would have taken about one hour in the States, took about three. Dr. Romero and the driver acted like we had all the time in the world to make this trip, and I decided I would just have to go with the flow.

Once we turned off into the mountains, the road changed. It was now unpaved and suddenly very steep and narrow, with many sharp corners on the edges of cliffs that dropped straight down. Most of the time there was mountainside right up against one side of the road and a sheer cliff face straight down on the other. And of course there were no guard rails, not that they would have done much good. I think the truck hung halfway over the side of the road when we went around curves. Once when passing another truck,

I looked out the window and I couldn't see the edge of the road, I just saw straight down, with no bottom in sight. The truck on the other side of the road must have been scraping against the side of the mountain. After that I just closed my eyes when we passed a truck. Somehow we finally arrived at the ranch. And, guess what! The ranch manager wasn't there. He had gone to Bacolod City! So we sat and waited.

Then it began to rain, and it looked like we were in for a good downpour. Turning around, the driver got the truck stuck in a deep ditch. Getting it out gave us something to do for a couple of hours. To top things off, the jeepney that had come with us had a flat tire, and there was no spare. Looking about, I could not begin to imagine where there would be a place to fix the tire, because we seemed to be in the middle of nowhere. Luckily, a person living nearby told us there was a repair shop about a kilometer away, so we jumped in the truck with the tire in the cab with us and headed out. I don't know why they didn't put the tire in the back of the truck. We drove for more than an hour — more than a kilometer obviously — finally arriving at a little town called Candoni that had a repair shop and a little restaurant with a dirt floor. It was not what you might imagine. It was a bamboo shack with a thatched roof, a large doorway with no door, and windows with no screens. Outside were the usual skinny swayback pig, skinny dogs, a couple of cats, and some chickens scratching about. It did not surprise me when a dog, cat, or chicken wandered inside. We had rice and fish for lunch, nothing unusual about that either.

On the way back to the ranch, our driver stopped at a pipe with water squirting out of it from somewhere up in the mountains. He said it was supposed to be safe to drink. I knew that was not always the case so I was a bit nervous about it. But I was also really thirsty and tired of drinking soda pop or beer, the two safest drinks. The water tasted so good, and I didn't get sick, so I guess it was all right. It was not very often I took such chances because the risk of illness was so great.

Meanwhile back at the ranch.... The ranch hands had decided to start rounding up the heifers we needed, even though it was still raining. When we drove back into the ranch, we could see them running barefoot over the steep mountainside, through the mud and rain, chasing the cattle. I was a little concerned about their safety as I watched men and cattle slipping and falling, but there wasn't much I could do, so I hung out in the dry truck. Finally in the late afternoon the rain stopped and I decided to walk around and stretch my legs, chatting a bit with an old woman – who could speak a little English – all the while watching the ranch hands cursing and covered with mud, as they chased those critters. The cattle were very different from our cows in the states. Of course they had four legs, but that was their only likeness. They all had a hump on their shoulders that came from breeding with Brahma cattle and were of many different colors with many indescribable markings. They were ornery, bad-tempered, good jumpers, and could out-run any man. They acted more like wild animals than domestic cattle. Then it began to rain again so I jumped back in the truck and I have no idea how they managed to finally get the cattle corralled. But they did around 5:30 in the evening. It was hard to believe that 14 hours had gone by since I had started on this trip. I was ready for this day to be over.

I gave a sigh of relief when the ranch manager finally arrived, but what happened next just blew my mind. He told the ranch hands that they had rounded up the wrong cattle! The right ones were already standing around in a large corral ready to be put into a smaller corral for loading into the truck. So another hour or so went by getting that group into the smaller corral so they could be loaded in the morning. It looked like we might get our heifers after all.

It was dark out and it seemed that we were finally finished for the day but wait, not yet. Even though it was dark, the wind was still blowing, it was still pouring rain, and the only light we had came from beer bottles filled with kerosene into which they stuffed and lit an old rag, we were told that the heifers must be branded. The ranch hands went straight to work building a fire, using one of the small corral's fences—which believe it or not was made out of an impervious jumble of all sorts of local material like sticks, brush, bamboo, old logs and boards all piled up – to heat the branding irons and keep themselves warm, since it was now downright cold. After more frenzy in the dark, two heifers were branded. It was amazing that they had gotten two done since they had no horses to ride and, no chutes to put the wild critters in. They had only ropes to do what seemed an impossible task. Only thirty-eight to go!

Since it was getting late, the ranch manager decided to call it a day. We would go to his house for food and sleep and would finish the job in the morning. I was tuckered out, cold, and hungry. Food and bed would feel good. The two men who had followed us in the jeepney didn't come with us. I have no idea where they spent the night.

We drove about half an hour to the manager's house, a wooden shack that looked very small for a family. We were given the typical warm welcome and it felt wonderful to get out of the rain and into a dry place. The house was dark, lit only by one beer-bottle lantern. We then sat around for an hour and talked, while my stomach wondered if there was any such thing as food on this cold mountaintop. Some more beer-bottle lanterns were brought in, and as the place became lighter, I noticed it was all black with soot. The flames from the lanterns went about a foot up in the air, along with black smoke, as the wind found its way in through the cracks in the sides of the house. That explained the soot. It seemed kind of dangerous, but since no one else seemed nervous, I relaxed as best I could. As my eyes adjusted to the semi-light, I began to see what was really in the room. All the time I had been there I had had a funny feeling that there was more to this party than met the eye. Sure enough, as my eyes adjusted, I could see twelve pairs of eyes staring at me. These belonged to the manager's children, who were sitting all around the room—in corners, under shelves, and in little crannies. They watched every move I made and sat so still that I wondered if they were really alive. I was probably the first American they had ever seen and I'm sure the first in their home. I suddenly felt like a giant who had invaded the home of these little people, who weren't sure what to do with me. After a while, they started moving around a little, always keeping me in their sight. It turned out that there were twelve children at home, three more off at school, and there was one who had died. That made sixteen in all, one for each year their parents had been married.

We had a very late supper of rice and more rice. Even though the father was a farm manager, the family was very poor. I was a little uncomfortable about their having three extra people for them to feed, but they were obviously very pleased to have us visiting them. Then they did the most amazing thing: they brought out a can of Campbell's pork and beans. They had probably been saving it for some special occasion; my visit seemed to be one. I felt honored. After supper we went to bed, since it was now very late. I was so tired I could have slept on just about anything and indeed that is what happened. As their guest, I was given the only bed they had. It was made out of split bamboo poles, with no mattress, no pillow, and no blanket. The bed was probably the parents', with the children sleeping on the floor, on mats that were rolled up during the day. I don't know where Dr. Romero and the truck driver slept.

I had expected it to be cooler up in the mountains, not cold. It didn't occur to me that I should bring a heavy jacket or my own blanket. So there I was, trying to make myself comfortable so I could sleep, as the rain made a racket on the tin roof and the wind rocked the cabin until I thought it would blow away. And it was really cold. I felt like I was going to freeze to death and had a hard time remembering that the Philippines was in the tropical weather zone. I started shivering and couldn't stop. I vaguely remembered that shivering was the body's way of keeping itself warm, so away I shivered through a restless sleep, looking forward to morning and heading home.

The next day went just about in the same frenzied manner as the first; trying to brand more heifers—notice I said trying – and getting the two branded ones onto the truck with a very long rope around the neck of the heifer and a number of men pulling as hard as possible, and some men waving their arms and yelling from behind but not too close, while the stubborn critter jumped, jerked and flailed wildly about as it was very slowly dragged to a ramp and up into the truck. It was very time-consuming getting those two critters loaded. We finally had our heifers and headed back down the mountain.

About midday I dragged myself into our house with the news. We had dropped off two heifers to two farmers. So it went in the Philippines.

A common sight on the road — Carabao and cart

In Bacolod City crowds would follow us, even at the beach.

Pinches, Giggles, and Crowds

MATTHEW – FALL, 1971

Here we go again, getting off a crowded rickety bus, being pushed along with the crowd out and into the already crowded city. When I rode on a bus or jeepney as a three-year-old, my world seemed to be a blur of people. Once off them, in Daddy's arms, I saw a sea of heads moving around me. On the ground, holding tight to his hand, I was surrounded by moving legs. Being so small, I felt safer when Daddy held me. Even though I was getting used to riding on buses and jeepneys, it was still a little scary getting off and going into crowds. I thought Daniel was very brave to ride on a jeepney alone. He was the only one allowed to.

This particular time, the whole family got off the bus. We had been on a trip and were back in Bacolod City. As we waited to cross the street, Daddy decided he had better do a head count. He was always counting us when we were in crowds, because he worried about one of us getting lost. Later we found out that kidnapping was also a threat, but we didn't know that then. It does explain, however, why Daddy and Mommy were always hanging on to us. But they never made it an issue then, and we never felt threatened as we traveled and moved about in strange and different places.

So Daddy started counting, "One, two, three; Daniel, Nancy, Peter." He stopped looked around and counted again, "One, two, three; Daniel, Nancy, Peter. Where is Matthew?" He looked at Mommy, who looked back at him wondering what the problem was. Daddy was looking really worried, and none of us could figure out why.

Finally I said, "Hi Daddy."

There I was in his arms, sitting on his hip, where I had been all along. Daddy just squeezed me tight and said, "How silly of me." We all got a good laugh over his "losing" me. He has never forgotten that day.

It was not always easy for us riding on the buses, because there were six of us and the buses were always very crowded. Sometimes there were no seats for us. When that happened people who did have seats often reached out to take Peter and me, because they wanted the little *"Cano"* boys to sit on their laps. Sometimes they even took Nancy, and she was a lot bigger. One time the bus was so crowded that we all had to stand until a man gave Mommy his seat. Both Peter and I then sat on her lap. Daddy was standing beside us all squished up, his head bending way over, like he was looking at his feet, because he was too tall for the low ceiling all the buses had. He looked funny standing that way, but I guess he didn't feel funny.

Filipinos were not used to an American family with four kids riding on their local buses. When I sat on someone's lap I was very quiet and kept my eyes glued on Mommy and Daddy, who were sometimes a few people away but had their eyes glued on me as well. Every now and then, Mommy would give me a reassuring smile as hands reached out to pinch my cheek. Mommy told me that meant they liked me. I didn't like it, and it hurt sometimes. I didn't like it either that they touched and sometimes ran their fingers through my hair. This happened a lot to Peter and me, who were blond, and even to Nancy, whose hair was long and light brown. Mommy said they touched our hair because it was so different from their own straight black hair, and they wanted to see what it felt like.

Everywhere we went as a family during our stay in Bacolod City, people stared at us. We were called *"Cano"* and often we could hear kids shouting *"Cano, Cano"* and pointing as they ran toward us. If we sat on a park bench, people of all ages gathered around us, coming closer and closer, wanting to talk to us, touch us, or just stare at us. And they giggled at lot. If I sneezed, they giggled. If Peter started jumping up and down or being silly, which he often did, they would giggle and point. If Nancy bent over to whisper something in Mommy's ear, or Daniel started teasing one of us, they giggled. Mommy said she sometimes felt like we were like animals in the zoo that people came to watch and laugh at. But she and Daddy were always friendly. If it got to be too much, they got us up and we went on our way, the crowd following for a while and then drifting off.

In the open markets the same thing happened: people followed us, tried to touch us, and laughed. Little kids stared at us from behind their parents. I held tight to my mother's hand and leaned a little closer to her. One time when we were shopping, Mommy stopped by a vendor who was sitting on a low stool, surrounded by baskets full of brooms and other household items. The brooms all had very short handles. When Mommy took one of them and tried sweeping with it, everybody around us laughed. I guess they thought that was funny, this tall American lady bending over trying to sweep. Mommy did buy the broom, because it was the only kind we could get for sweeping our floors. But she couldn't find a dust mop.

Even on some of the beaches, we attracted a crowd. As we walked along the beach, Mommy showing us different shells and other things of interest, people watched us, giggled at us, listened to us, and touched us if they got close enough. And many followed us. When that happened, Mommy just kept walking and talking to us, and she always had a smile for those following us. We did not get to go swimming because the beaches were dirty and there was often garbage coming in on the waves. If we found a beach that was fairly clean, Mommy would let us wade in the water for a little bit. About the only clean beaches were private. Private beaches were very hard to find. You had to get invited to some of them and there were others where you had to pay. On our Peace Corps allowance, we could not afford this. I never felt we were poor. I do not think Daniel, Nancy, or Peter thought we were poor. We were not poor like most of the people living around as. But I guess people in the United States would have thought we were.

Of course the people surrounding us talked about us. I don't know what they were saying, because I couldn't understand their language. Neither could Mommy and Daddy. And anyone who could wanted to speak English with us. But we were definitely curiosities. Except for Peace Corps Volunteers, most Americans and other foreigners, and wealthy Filipinos, had their own cars and shopped in grocery or department stores. They had maids who did the shopping in the open markets, and Americans and other "white people" swam at private beaches.

So we were very different; not only from them, but from other Americans they had seen or known. Until now they had seen single Peace Corps Volunteers mingling with, living with, and working with them. But they had never seen a Peace Corps family up close, being a real part of their lives. So while it was all very different for us, it was also different for them.

We saw many beaches like this.

The bathroom in our home in Baguio

Dirty Bathrooms and Precious Water

PETER – 1971-1973

Daniel and I jumped off the crowded bus, Daniel calling, "Race you to the bathroom, Peter," as we ran ahead of Daddy, Mommy, Nancy, and Matthew. We really had to go. We were on our way home from a long day trip and it seemed like we had been on the bus for hours. It hadn't stopped because it had not broken down. A woman had let her baby pee on the floor. Mommy reminded us that some families were so poor they couldn't afford diapers. I wondered what would happen if a baby had to poop. Daddy has told you, in "Wild Rides," about how the buses were always breaking down, how we said they were held together with rubber bands and bubblegum. But one thing the frequent breakdowns did provide was bathroom breaks. When a bus broke down, people would get off and go pee in the bushes. The girls went to one side of the road and the boys to the other. Sometimes that was the only chance you had for hours.

On one of our bus rides, we actually stopped where there was a bathroom. Daniel and I really had to go, so we raced to the bathroom and quickly put on our brakes at the open door: a gross smell was coming out. We had been in a few bathrooms that were rundown looking, dirty and smelly, with no toilet paper or sinks, but this one seemed worse. We decided to wait for Daddy, who told us it was okay, that it was not much different from a number he had been in. We weren't happy as we looked around, but if Daddy said okay, we decided it must be. I was going to pee fast and get out. I passed the toilets that didn't have a seat or lid, some with tanks also without lids. There were no doors either. I tried not to look when I saw a man standing on the toilet and squatting down to poop. And there was a man washing his hands in the tank on the back of the toilet. One toilet was broken. I was sure glad I didn't have to poop: I could barely pee because of the smell. Daniel and I got done really fast and ran out of the bathroom holding our noses. As we came out, Nancy was coming out of the girls' room. She wasn't holding her nose; she just had an unhappy look on her face. She told us about peeing in a dirty toilet that Mommy would not let her sit on. Mommy held Matthew up over the toilet so he could pee. And the sinks were dirty and some were broken. We decided it was better to pee in the bushes. Now we really understood why Mommy and Daddy avoided using public bathrooms as much as possible. Mommy always had a damp washcloth with her to wash us off and Daddy always carried along a roll of toilet paper.

Mommy still tells one of our favorite bathroom stories. We had been on one of our bus trips and stopped at a *sari sari* store – *sari sari* means "variety" in Tagalog – the national language. Some really were sorry-looking, with only three sides and a dirt floor, and they smelled awful. There were some that were clean and looked like nice little markets, but we didn't see them very often, The stores carried a variety of things, like hats, cigarettes, batteries, pickled eggs, and other snack foods that Mommy would never let us buy because she never knew if they were safe or not. They also had warm soda pop and candy, which we could sometimes buy. Daniel liked the bigger *sari sari* stores because they sold firecrackers, and some sold a variety of wooden statues – mostly of carabaos, woven baskets, and other art objects. *Sari sari* stores were everywhere in the cities and countryside. Unlike in the United States, however, there were no gas pumps there. Nobody in my family can remember where the buses or jeepneys got gas. Daddy had to fill up his motor scooter on occasion, but the rest of us never saw a gas station because we didn't have a car.

Back to Mommy and her story. She disappeared behind the store and when she came back she said, "You won't believe what just happened. The bathroom was smelly, as usual, and it had a narrow concrete slab on the floor going from one wall to the other. It had a little skinny ditch running through the middle with water trickling through it. Along the little ditch on each side of it were little places the size of a shoe for your feet. They were just a little bit higher than the concrete. Well, I put a foot on each little step so I was standing over the little ditch. I stood over it and started peeing and heard this slurp, gurgle, slurp, gurgle, slop noise. I looked over to where the ditch with water and my pee were running out of the building through a little hole in the wall, and I couldn't believe it when I saw a little yellow bill poking through the wall happily slurping and drinking that water. Can you believe that?" We all immediately headed behind the store. There was the building and behind it the ducks with little yellow bills happily slurping about in the muddy yuck. What could we say?

In our home, Mommy kept the bathroom nice and clean, but sometimes we didn't have water in our house and couldn't flush the toilet or use the sink or shower. When we lived in Bacolod City and that happened Mommy would have to haul water from the outside pump. She was always getting after Daddy about remembering to pump water up into the tower so we would have water in the house. We sometimes took our baths outside at the pump, because it was easier than in the house. It was also great fun in that hot climate to splash around in the water and wash our hair outside. I liked to climb the water tower and one day I fell off of it. I landed on the concrete on my back. It about scared me to death, but while I was sore, I wasn't really hurt. Mommy said it was good the water tower was only about twelve feet tall or I might not have been so lucky.

We really had to be careful with our water, and Mommy always boiled our drinking water. It seemed like she spent a lot of time boiling water. Mommy was always figuring out ways to reuse our water and was always careful how much she used. She said water was precious. When we brushed our teeth she would give us a cup of water to use and that was it. When the water was off in Baguio she put one of our washtubs in the shower and had us sit or stand in it. She would haul a bucket of water from the storage trailer and pour it over us, tell us to soap up, and would pour another bucket over us to get the soap off. Any water that collected in the washtub we were standing in was used by the next person if it wasn't very dirty, and Mommy decided that. She firmly believed in reusing! In Baguio we didn't bathe outside because there wasn't a place to do it and, besides, it was often much cooler than Bacolod City. Baguio was high in the mountains. Bacolod was in the hot flatland. I was sure glad when we moved from there. I didn't like the hot weather at all.

While in the Philippines we got used to seeing people bathing, going to the bathroom, or washing their clothes in all kinds of places. Our neighbor would get up early in the morning and step out on his little back porch and pee right there on the ground. Sometimes the smell from that house would come right into ours. We would drive through a little village and see people bathing near the edge of the dirt road, where there was public water available. The grownups could take a bath and somehow keep themselves wrapped up so you never saw them naked. Mommy got pretty good at that too. She could get in and out of a bathing suit and into her clothes wrapped in a towel. We saw naked kids all over the place, and they would just squat down anyplace to pee and poop. When we traveled near rivers we often saw women washing their clothes and laying them out on rocks to dry. Mommy was glad she didn't have to do that. It was hard enough washing all our clothes by hand in our washtubs. I didn't like helping to wash clothes. I liked playing in the water better, which is mainly what I would do when I was supposed to be helping.

Not all Filipinos were that poor. Many used bathrooms and bathed indoors. Some hired people to do their laundry in their house. Some of the wealthier had washing machines and other modern conveniences. But we didn't get to know very many people like that. And you know, I can't remember the bathrooms in our schools. Maybe they were more like what we were used to in the United States. I just know I did my share of peeing outside when I was in the Philippines.

A roadside sari sari store

Christmas carolers/dancers

Christmas, Firecrackers, and New Year's

DANIEL – DECEMBER 1971

Christmas came, that first year, and aside from the fact that the weather was hot instead of cold, the big issue was: what were we going to do about a tree? We had always hiked out in the woods and cut our own. We knew that we could not afford to buy one—even a fake one, which Daddy would never have tolerated, and we knew, too, that we had no decorations even if we had a tree. Aside from Matthew, who had only a hazy recollection of Christmas, we children couldn't imagine a Christmas without one.

With Matthew solemnly watching us, as he so often did, we confronted Mommy. We wanted a tree and didn't want any argument. We weren't feeling very friendly toward our parents or the Philippines at the moment, so we grumbled and complained while Mommy stood and listened, never saying a word.

"We can't even bake Christmas cookies," groaned Nancy. "We don't have an oven."

"Why were they singing "I'm Dreaming of a White Christmas" in this country in October?" I demanded.

"Santa probably won't even find us here. Does he know we moved here?" asked Peter.

"Who's Santa?" Matthew muttered.

"I don't know why we came to this country anyway. All the people do is stare at us or laugh at us or pinch us. I don't like it," Peter said, as he stomped his foot.

"I miss Grandma and Grandpa." Nancy was close to tears.

"Will we have presents?" Peter wondered.

"Don't be silly Peter of course we will have presents." Nancy answered him.

"I just think it stinks that we won't have a tree." I said.

Mommy heard us out and then said, "Look guys, I know you're upset and it doesn't seem fair, and you don't like the pinches. I don't either, and I miss Grandma and Grandpa too. But don't worry. Santa will come, we will have Christmas, and no, we won't have a tree, but we will work something out. Maybe we'll figure out a way to make one. Now, if you guys are through here I need to boil some water. Okay?" Feeling a little less angry, we let it drop for the moment.

"They'll get a tree somehow won't they?" asked Peter, as we headed out of the house.

"No! They won't Peter," snapped Nancy.

"But, they'll figure something out," I assured them. "Like Mommy said, maybe we'll make one"

Our gloom did not last long. Just as we do in the US, Filipinos love Christmas. Before long we were swept up into the Christmas spirit, little knowing some of the new and exciting things we would encounter all the way through to the new year. It turned out that we were too busy to be homesick and even the Christmas tree fell into the background. As Nancy often said, "It was the same, but different."

The holiday started off with a big bang—literally. As Christmas approached, we heard firecrackers everywhere. Homemade bamboo cannons boomed, along with other types of noisemakers. Boom! Boom! Day after day. This was something I could relate to and I set off a few firecrackers myself.

Just like in the States, we did the usual school Christmas programs, with one big difference. Filipinos love to visit and talk with one another, so while everybody was waiting for the shows to start the people in the audience talked, visited, and wandered around. The difference was that they didn't stop once the program began. During the performance and the speeches, the crowd kept on talking and moving about. Mommy said she thought they all acted like Americans at a football game. I don't know about that, but they were noisy, and it did make it hard to hear.

Our wealthy neighbors, the Sarmientos, invited us to go with them to their church to see the Christmas cantata. Although I didn't look forward to it, I have to admit they put on a good show, called "The Night the Angels Sang." The chorus sang beautifully, and the children who played Mary, Joseph, and the Wise Men acted with great feeling and were really into the Christmas spirit. But once again, the congregation just kept talking when the program started. It wasn't until the priest told everybody to pray that they finally kept quiet.

Another thing I couldn't help but notice in that church was that there were bird droppings on the rafters and elsewhere. It being a hot country and there being no air conditioning, the church doors were left open much of the time, and there were no screen doors. So, according to Nancy and the evidence, birds flew around and in and out of the building during the day.

And then there was the smell. The Philippines is actually a pretty smelly country in many places because the sanitation is so poor. The heat and humidity make it worse. When we lived in cooler Baguio the smells were not "in your face" nearly so much. Part of the problem was that men, boys, and small children were not very choosy about where they peed. Little kids often just squatted down right where they were to take a leak. And you already know about the bathrooms. So even in the church you could smell the mixture of dirt and pee. The smells were hard to get used to, but we had to; there was no choice.

During the holidays, we went to three family parties. The first one was a couple of weeks before Christmas, given by the Bureau of Animal Industry for their workers and families. For it we took a boat and went overnight to the island of Panay to Iloilo City. Panay is just west and not far from the island Negros Occidental, where we lived. In the Philippines the definition of "family" was very broad, so there were lots of people of all ages visiting and enjoying each other.

The party began with contests for the children. First they had a singing contest. Of course the group wanted us to sing a song too, and finally Nancy, Peter, and I gave in and sang a Christmas carol. Nancy also sang a song by herself. Next was a reciting contest. I tried to get out of that one, but ended up reciting a poem after Nancy did one. Now I knew why in school they made us memorize and recite poetry. The next event was right up my alley. They had a banana-eating contest— again for kids. Of course Peter and Nancy joined in. I started gobbling down the bananas like I hadn't eaten in a week. I was sure I could win this contest, but would you believe a tiny little Filipino kid, who made me look like a giant, beat me by one banana. He ate five bananas in three minutes to my four.

Then it was time for the adults. Some groups sang Christmas carols; a few individuals sang songs and some did Filipino folk dances. The folk dances were always fun to watch because the dancers were really in to it. Nancy, Peter, and I had learned a few of them ourselves during Peace Corps training. I wasn't much for the dancing but Mommy and Nancy loved it. I did like the one dance called the Tinikling where you had to jump in and out of two bamboo poles that were being slapped against each other and against the floor in time to the music. It wasn't easy to do, and if you weren't quick you got your ankle whacked. The Filipinos were really good at it, and Nancy and I got pretty good. I have to admit, though, Nancy was better than I.

After all that it was time to eat, and the people hit the food like a pack of starving dogs. There were no lines, no order, just people pushing and shoving and filling their plates. Mommy and Daddy took us back to our seats and made us wait for the crowd to thin out. As a result, we hardly got anything to eat. There was more singing and dancing after the meal and then we were off to spend the night with our Peace Corps regional representative and his family. That was a treat for us because they had a really nice house, similar to one in the States, with modern conveniences that reminded me of how shabby and small ours was.

The next day we headed home, returning the way we had come. The jeepney ride from the dock was one wild trip. A jeepney normally held 14 people, but this driver was determined to cram 28 and their baggage into his. The more people he took, the more money he made. The driver seemed worried about where the six of us were going. He and Daddy talked and reached some sort of agreement, because Daddy said that there were no other jeepneys going our way and he did not want to wait around. He never liked to have to wait and he was always up to the big challenge, which in this case was getting all those people into the jeepney. Somehow it was done. There were kids and baggage sitting on adults, baggage in the aisle, and baggage and a couple of men hanging off the back. I was crammed in the front of the jeepney next to the driver and two other people. I could barely see out. The rest of the family was crammed into the back, along with everyone and everything else. That jeepney was riding right low to the ground. Off we went at up to 25 to 35 miles an hour over the dirt road, hitting every pothole and rocking to and fro, our brains and insides jiggling about. Along the way we dropped off a few people, but when our stop came, we still had an awful lot of baggage and people to clamber over to get out. We still were not home. Rather frazzled, we soon caught another jeepney that was just about empty and finally got home.

About a week before Christmas, carolers started coming. I had never seen so many. Some were groups of children, some were adults. They came in the evening, often right up until nine or ten. They wore colorful clothes, the girls often in long dresses, and sang and sometimes danced for us, balancing candles in little glasses on the palms of their hands and sometimes on their heads. That was a very beautiful dance.

Along with the carolers came the beggars. They had no songs to sing: they just wanted anything you could give. One came with her baby and a companion who was pregnant. While they stood, hands out, the baby peed on our porch. Like many babies in this country, he was not wearing a diaper. We gave them some money and they left. Immediately Matthew got a pitcher and dumped two loads of water over the porch. Then there was an old man who was collecting bottles and jars to sell. He was willing to pay us a little for them. Of course we just gave him the bottles, which made his eyes shine. Some of the carolers also expected us to give them money.

When Christmas Eve was — finally — only a couple days away, we were pretty excited. We had made Christmas chains out of colored paper and had sent Christmas cards we had made, just as we did in the States. We bought some handmade Filipino decorations and some Christmas lights. Mommy put a nativity scene she had bought and a few decorations on a low table against the wall. Not the same as at home, but pretty Christmasy. We all were wondering what Santa was going to bring us: we hadn't got any toys since we had arrived, back in June. We were ready! Of course that close to Christmas, we wondered again how we would deal with that Christmas tree problem. Mommy and Daddy had not said anything, so neither did we.

It was finally Christmas Eve and we were off to the Sea Breeze Hotel, to the Christmas party for the employees. We had loved it there and were really excited. The hotel was all decorated with beautiful things that the staff had made. All the staff we knew were there, with their families. We were seated at the head table with the owner's family, an honor we had not expected. The main event of the evening was Filipino dances, performed by different members of the staff. The women wore Filipino dresses, and the men had on dark pants and embroidered white shirts. They looked cool, and the dances were fun to watch. The Tinikling–with those bamboo poles – was always a favorite at gatherings. The women in the laundry department did the best dance. They were grandmotherly women who were obviously enjoying themselves as they kicked up their heels and swung about. The owner's children also performed. Thank goodness we didn't have to! The partying was going to last until mass at midnight, but we left at ten o'clock. We were so tired we could hardly hold our eyes open during the jeepney ride home. We hung up our stockings, looked at the colored lights surrounding the nativity scene, glanced at the presents under the little table the scene was on, and fell into bed, wondering if Santa would come.

"Daniel, Daniel, are you awake?" whispered Nancy early the next morning.

"Huh, yah I'm awake," I yawned.

"Quick, get Peter and I'll get Matthew so we can wake Mommy and Daddy," she whispered.

Then the four of us went and piled on our parents' bed. The rule was that we could not go into the living room until they were up and ready. Daddy opened his eyes and gave us a big grin, and Mommy buried her head under her pillow.

"Hurry, hurry!" we all shouted, jumping up and down on the bed. "Come on Mommy, it's time to get up."

Suddenly Daddy grabbed Peter and got him in a headlock, and Peter grabbed my leg, pulling me down on top of them. I pushed Nancy, who fell on Daddy's head, and Matthew jumped on top of the pile. Mommy peeked out from under her pillow and said it was time to see what Santa brought – before she was pulled onto the pile. We all unscrambled and, with our parents first, as was the tradition, we went into the living room.

He had come! Santa had found us in the Philippines! Our stockings were full, and standing there, bright and new, were three bikes for us bigger kids and a big yellow Tonka truck for Matthew. For a couple of hours, we were the typical American family enjoying Christmas morning. Suddenly there was a knock at the door, and there was our friend Mr. Arceo, who invited us to join his family for their Christmas gathering. So once again we became part of another crowd of relatives and more relatives, with singing, dancing, games, and eating that would go on until ten or eleven at night. We were used to these parties by now and were really into the swing of things. We even participated in the children's programs. It's not so hard to recite a poem or sing a song when that is what the other children are doing and nobody laughs or makes fun of you for doing it. We left the party in the middle of the afternoon, when the gambling games began. We wanted to get home and ride our bikes.

Before we went to the family gathering, we did have one other thing to do. It was during the Christmas holidays that the terrible poverty that existed here really hit all of us hard. Here was a holiday that was joyous, and so many people seemed caught up in it, yet underneath it all were the millions of people who had nothing. We made up three packages of food and toys for three very needy families in our neighborhood, whose children we played with and who barely had a roof over their heads. Christmas morning we headed across the dusty fields and dirty creek to give them our gifts. You would have thought we had dropped out of heaven, the way they thanked us over and over. It seemed such a small thing to do, but it had a big impact.

About the Christmas tree. We did not have a Christmas tree. Christmas Eve, while nobody was around and before we went to the party at the hotel, Mommy had hung the chains we'd made and the Christmas lights on the wall and brought them down to the outside edge of the little table where the nativity scene sat. On the wall where the chains and lights came together, she placed a star. When we got back from the party, she turned on the lights. The triangle of colorful lights and homemade chains was just beautiful. Mommy had captured Christmas and brought us a tree.

Between Christmas and New Year's, our home became the gathering place for a number of very poor Filipino kids from the neighborhood whom we had not seen before. Some just came and stood by the road and watched us. Some climbed in the guava tree in the back yard and watched us, while helping themselves to the guava fruit that they would take home. Mommy tried to get the ones stealing the fruit to stop, but that was a lost cause and she soon gave up. They needed the fruit more than we did. I don't know why these kids suddenly started coming. Usually our little street and neighborhood was pretty quiet, with just a few kids about. Was it because we had taken food to some, or because everybody was on Christmas break? I have no idea. The boy next door, whom I hardly ever saw, actually came into our yard around then and we played and I got to know him. We made a nifty volcano out of mud. It was at least two feet tall. It was hollow in the center with a hole at the top so we could build a real fire in it. It was pretty cool watching sparks and smoke come out of the top, about a foot in the air. One day he came over and had a large, dirty scrape on his arm. I took him to Mommy and she cleaned the scrape and bandaged it up. Now that caused quite the sensation as he proudly showed the arm that the *"Cano"* had bandaged to everybody. I don't know what his family thought of it. They never came around even though they were right next door, except for the times early on, when one of the women who lived there squatted by the fence and watched us.

A couple of times some boys came into the house and played with our Christmas toys. I guess that was a big deal for them, since they had so little. But the thing they all liked best was riding our bikes. That turned out to be a disaster, because some could not ride very well and some were careless with them. Daddy, Peter, and I had some fixing to do. None of the kids who caused the damage ever apologized or helped us fixed them. They just acted like it was the way things were. They just didn't seem to care and I guess they didn't.

Finally New Year's Eve came. It was different from anything we had ever seen. Remember those pre-Christmas firecrackers I told you about? We hadn't seen anything yet. New Year's Eve people started setting off firecrackers and anything else that made a loud noise and lots of sparks and smoke. The whole area smelled like it was on fire. It looked like the whole neighborhood and

Bacolod City in the distance was a war zone. Smoke was billowing into the air over the city and the explosions were ear-shattering. When we went to bed it was all still going strong. We could not sleep, so we got up and watched all the commotion that now seemed crazy and almost scary. After midnight things slowly started quieting down, and we were finally able to sleep. What a way to end the year!

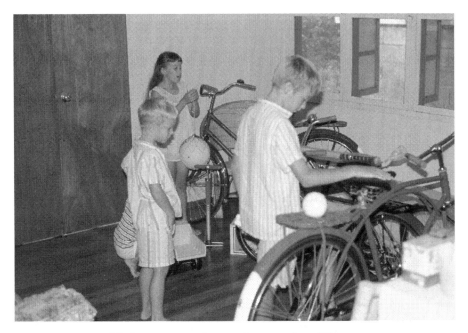

Christmas morning — the same but different

Sugar cane going to the sugar central

Poverty and SugarCane

NANCY – APRIL 1972

My brothers and I were excited because we were going to visit Delia's family and tour a sugar factory, called a sugar central in the Philippines. We loved to go on trips, even though Daddy said they were "educational." Sometimes we groaned when Daddy got started on his educational stuff, but most of the time we actually had fun. The great part about this trip was we wouldn't have to take the public bus. Since Daniel's best friend, Andre, was coming with us, Andre's father was letting us use his VW bus and driver for the day, which would make the trip lots easier and faster. We weren't the only ones going. Delia was, of course, since we were going to visit her family. This was a really big deal for Delia and her family and again, like with Terry, Delia felt comfortable enough with us to invite us to her home and to feel we would not make her feel ashamed because of her poor living conditions. Then there was our good friend Caesar; he loved our family and since moving to Bacolod City, he visited a lot and would often go places with us. I think he thought he had to take care of us. One thing for sure, he was always a help with the language. Delia's family didn't speak English and she was slowly picking it up.

So, off all ten of us went. We loved being in a private vehicle From Bacolod City we drove up the coast to Victorias, where Delia lived. The road was flat and partially paved. Along the way we saw miles and miles of sugar cane fields. Sugar cane has a thick stalk, like corn, and leaves that look a little like corn leaves. It is very tall.

Some of the fields were on fire. Sugar cane stalks don't burn and the fires, which burned all the rest of the plant, made them easier to cut down and protected the workers from the cane's very sharp leaves. In some of the fields, men were cutting down the sugar cane stalks with large machetes. What a hard job out in those hot fields! Everything was black from the fires, and in addition to the heat and hard work, the workers were covered with soot. We also saw big trucks, which were loaded by hand, hauling cane to the sugar central.

What was really fascinating was watching boys running behind the trucks, trying to grab pieces of sugar cane off the back. It was very dangerous, and they weren't supposed to do it. But they were hungry, and the sugar cane stalk is sweet and juicy, a real treat for children who didn't have much.

We finally came to the village where Delia lived. It was on a strip of land on which, over the years, squatters had built their houses, turning it into a village of sorts. It was a place that did not get many visitors. There were houses crammed together between the main road and a river that ran into the ocean. It was nothing like where Terry, Mommy's co-worker, lived, and we'd thought that village was poor! The river had tides, because it was near the ocean, which meant that the ground under the stilt houses was covered with water when the tide was up, twice a day. Some of the houses already had water around and under them. Delia told us that when it rained, the whole area flooded and when there was a bad storm, their homes flooded. What a way to have to live!

We left the VW and driver on the road, since there were no streets in the village, and walked in. There were no lawns, no grass, no flowers, just black mud and trash, and that now-familiar urine smell. There were narrow walkways with wooden planks between the houses, which were so close together they almost touched. It was like going through a narrow maze. Clotheslines hung from house to house, some across our path, some out over the edge of the river. There were little ditches filled with dirty black water and more trash, men sitting with the roosters that they took to cockfights—lots of people sitting around and lots of children. We were being watched from every window and by everybody outside. Every now and then, somebody would reach out to touch one of us. Even after being here for almost a year, we were not used to living in a place where my brothers and I were always such oddities. But having "*Canos*" visit this village had probably never happened before. In addition, we were a family with four kids coming to visit one of their families. As we got closer to Delia's house a crowd gathered around us.

Delia's house, like all the houses, was on stilts and made out of wood and leaves from the nipa plant, with a metal roof. It looked pretty shaky, and it was hard to believe that it could support a second story, where another family lived. I never saw how that family got up there. The steps we climbed to get into the first floor were pretty rickety, and when we got into the house and walked on the floor, it shook. One of the walls was so loosely connected to the floor that you could see the ground between the floor and wall. As I looked down, I thought it must look pretty awful when the tide was up with all the trash and garbage floating about in the dirty river water.

I knew Delia's house would be small, but this house was tiny. It had only three rooms – if you can call the kitchen a room. It looked more like a double closet. I peeked in and saw what I was beginning to realize was a very typical kitchen for the poor. On the wooden counter there was an open fire pit built out of some type of metal, where the food was cooked. The family needed wood for the fire, of course, but I don't know if they collected it or bought it. The smoke went up to the ceiling and out. Next to the stove, with a little wall between them, was the dishwashing area – a metal pan sunk into the counter alongside a large urn with a spigot that held the water. I don't know where they got the water. When the washing was finished, they dumped the water right onto the ground. There were a few shelves. The kitchen walls and ceiling were black from all the smoke. The house smelled like a damp campfire.

The small living room, which was also where they ate, was between the kitchen and the bedroom. There was not much furniture—a wooden couch, a small dining table, and three or four chairs. While we were there, they made a bench for us to sit on out of a board and a couple of wooden crates. The bedroom was only about six feet by four feet, according to Daddy. It had nothing in it, not even a bed. I don't know where they kept their clothes. Delia said she and her parents, along with her five-year-old brother and seven-year-old sister, slept on the floor on bedding that was unrolled at bedtime. Her 16-year-old brother slept in the living room on the wooden couch. There was no toilet, no electricity, no refrigerator, and no running water. I didn't dare ask where they went to the bathroom.

The walls were made of brown paper and were decorated with a few pictures from magazines and some they'd drawn themselves. There were also a few statues around the house: a wooden carabao, and the Virgin Mary and Jesus. And like most of the homes we visited, whether poor or rich, there was a crucifix hanging on the wall. Despite the poverty, Delia's home was neat and clean, and the floor was shiny with wax, just the way Delia kept our floor at home.

It was hard for me to believe six people lived in this tiny little house and to realize that this was the way millions of Filipinos lived. No wonder Delia, as an 18-year-old, loved having her own bedroom at our place. No wonder it was so important that she could work for us and have some money to give to her parents. Our house, which was not big, must have seemed like a castle to her.

I thought it was really nice that Delia had invited us to spend some time with her family. However, we were not there long when we became bored. My brothers and I couldn't wander about outside because there was no place to go. We could practically reach out the window, which had no glass or screen, and touch the next house and there wasn't anything to do in the house but just sit on the bench. There were no toys and Delia's little brother and sister just stared at us with their shy smiles. I have no idea what they were thinking about all of this. My parents decided that we should go visit the sugar central while Delia and her mother made lunch. We were glad to get out of there.

The sugar central was really big. Daddy had been afraid we might not get in, because of rules about visitors, but we did, and we saw how brown and white sugar were made from the stalks and bagged up to go to stores. In one room the stalks were run through giant rollers, to squeeze out the sweet, juicy liquid. There were lots of steps to help crystallize the liquid. The most important one was putting it into a centrifuge that turned at an incredibly high speed. The most awesome thing for us was the building where there were bulldozers pushing the sugar into big piles of white and brown sugar — actual bulldozers! Big ones, I mean really big ones! We learned that the sugar from this central was going to Safeway supermarkets in the United States. We saw bags of "Candi Cane Sugar," with red and white candy canes on them. Mommy was almost sure she could remember seeing that brand back home.

After visiting the sugar central, we headed back to Delia's. We ate our meal, with crowds of people outside continuing to stare and giggle and point, practically hanging in the doorway and windows. Mommy had brought along some food, with Delia's approval, for she didn't want to offend the family. She knew Delia's mother would offer us more than they could really afford. Delia's mom appreciated the food but didn't include it as part of the meal. The meal consisted of rice, the usual soda pop, since the water was unsafe, bananas, dried squid, hardboiled eggs, and a couple of dishes of a mixed vegetables in some type of gravy. We were all happy — two families having a good time together. For a little while we were able to bridge the gap between us and find the ways we were the same.

Clothes along the river and the path to Delia's house

Nipa hut kitchen stove; to the right, out of the photo, is the sink and water urn

Delia and Frances getting ready to share a meal.
Note the walls lined with brown paper.

I made it to the top.

Leeches, Rain, and A Volcano

DANIEL - MAY 1972

I could not believe it when Daddy said we were going to climb Mount Canlaon, an 8,087 foot, inactive volcano on our island of Negros Occidental. I was relieved to hear it was not considered an active volcano, even though it did expel smoke now and then. There was no way as a twelve-year-old that I had the courage to climb an active one. This one was challenging enough. Mommy wondered who "we" meant. I think she was a little concerned, since "we" often meant the whole family, and she was not comfortable with that. "We" turned out to be Daddy and Mommy, our friend Bob — also a Peace Corps Volunteer — two guides, and me. Mommy and Daddy arranged for Nancy, Peter, and Matthew to stay with some friends for the day, and the rest of us were off to climb a volcano. We had to leave at 3:00 in the morning to be able to hike the volcano in one day. The night before we left, I was so excited I could hardly sleep. At 3:00 a.m. we were in the car, ready to go. The drive seemed to last forever, but we finally arrived at the base of Mount Canlaon, where we met our two local guides, who were to lead us to the top.

The volcano looked very steep and its forest as thick as a jungle. The rainfall there was quite heavy, so the whole area was damp and muggy. I could hardly believe that we were going to make it to the top, but I was ready to get started. We hiked up a small road into the forest for a while. Then we left the road and headed straight into the forest. I had butterflies in my stomach because now I felt our hike was starting for real. But where was the trail? We didn't see one, and the climb was really steep. Our guides, however, were not worried. They had been up the volcano many times and knew the way. They told us the trail was always overgrown with brush because the foliage grew so fast. They pulled out machetes — large, slightly curved, and very sharp knives — and began to cut through the brush, telling us to follow. They led us, following streams and ridges, hacking away at the dense underbrush, literally making a trail as we hiked. I wished I had a machete so I could help.

The climb kept getting more and more difficult and I was beginning to wonder if I would make it. We had been hiking for three hours and were still a long way from the top. The air had become very damp and hot and the ground very slippery. I slipped a lot, getting dirty, hot, and sweaty. After we had been hiking for about five hours we stopped for lunch by a nice stream. I was glad because I had to admit I was tired. However, being 12, I didn't rest long. I ran around and generally goofed off. Then I looked down and I saw a black, slimy thing on my leg. I tried to move it, but it would not budge. On my other leg was another one, and I noticed others silently moving up my legs. Somewhat freaked out, I ran to my parents, who were pretty calm as they told me they looked like leeches and not to pull them off. Mommy, always curious and never having seen a leech on land, sat there observing them for a few seconds before taking me to the guides to see how to get them off. Nobody told me there were going to be leeches on this hike. I thought leeches lived in water. The guides told us the leeches were harmless, that they could live on the volcano because it was always so wet and damp. Then they informed us that you simply burned the leech off. I suddenly felt very weak. I held my leg up, ready to scream bloody murder if I got burned. But it was no big deal. The guide held a lit match to the end of each stuck leech and they dropped off quickly. After that I decided to stay on the trail when we stopped. Lunch was over, and we were off again. It was getting hotter and the air was so damp that my clothes were beginning to feel like they had just come out of the washer.

The hike was tiring and it didn't help that every thirty seconds I kept looking down at my legs for leeches.

As we got closer to the top, the climb became steeper and harder and I was having my doubts about all of this. I was tired of the forest and of worrying about leeches, and was happy when we finally walked out into a steep, grassy field, strewn with volcanic rocks. Up ahead the peak was coming into view. We were almost there! As we approached the top, the sky darkened and a low mist and clouds floated across the grass towards us. This did not look good. I had worked hard to get this far and didn't want the weather to keep me from getting to the top. We kept climbing, the peak was getting quite near, and I was thinking that maybe this would all be worth it. Behind me, I could see the flatlands spreading out from the mountain's base — a beautiful sight. Mommy, rather damp and bedraggled, watched everything going on around her, finding it hard to believe she was near the top of a volcano. The guides, who always kept an eye on Mommy, seemed amazed that she had made it this far. They acted like they had never taken a "*Cano*" woman up with them, and they had probably expected her to complain. They sure didn't know my mother.

We left the field behind, entering a very steep slope, all covered with loose volcanic rock, crushed and slippery. Ridges of hard lava with loose rocks flowed down from the peak, looking like long, high tree roots. It was one of these ridges that we had to climb to reach the top. The ridge was about 18 inches wide, very steep, and very slippery from all the loose rock on it; and both sides dropped off rather steeply—hundreds of feet, looking like cliffs to me. I kept looking over the side, afraid I might fall at any time. The clouds and mist were continuing to roll in as light rain started, making the ridge even slipperier. Suddenly I fell. I was sure I was going to slide down the slope and be lost forever. My heart was thumping and my stomach went into a tight knot. As I scrambled to get my footing back, I wondered what I was doing here and why I had ever wanted to come. Shakily I regained my footing and we carefully moved on.

Despite the leeches, my slips, falls, worries, and the clouds, mist, and rain, we at last made it to the peak! It was wonderful. We could see through the mist down to the flatlands spread out below, dotted with little farms and towns. On the other side, we could see into the crater of the volcano, full of jumbled up piles of rock — not very scary anymore. Around the crater was a crumbled ridge, the remains of the cone. We were on the tallest part of the crater lip, with a very steep drop down into the crater. Neat! It was too steep to climb down into the crater and I was okay with that. I was just proud that I had made it to the top. But we weren't finished yet. We still had to go back down, and it was getting late.

The clouds were beginning to engulf us so the guides decided we needed to get off the ridge and head back down while we could still see. Soon we could hardly see ahead of us because the mist was so heavy, and it was beginning to rain. I was scared coming down the narrow, slippery ridge and once again wondered what I was doing up on this volcano. My relief at getting off the ridge and back on to the field did not last long. Now we had a thunderstorm to deal with. The wind lashed us, rain poured down by the bucketloads, and lighting and thunder blazed and roared across the mountain. A few times the lighting and thunder were so close together that I was sure they would strike us dead. I huddled closer to my parents, my stomach in a tight knot as I held back tears. This was more frightening than the leeches or falling off the ridge.

Going down the mountain was faster than going up, and we were soon into the steamy woods and out of the storm. By then, it was beginning to get dark. The ground was so muddy that we slid more than we walked. My parents and I spent most of the time on our behinds and were soon covered with mud. Mommy and Daddy kept assuring me that everything would be fine, that we would soon be back to the base. I wasn't so sure. My parents and I stuck close together so we would not lose each other. Mommy was holding my hand so tightly I thought it was going to fall off. I don't know what Bob was doing, I guess staying close to the guides, the only people not bothered by all of this.

We eventually reached the more level ground and knew we did not have much farther to go. But it was dark now and we were in for our last scary surprise. The guides lost the trail we were on! I vowed on the spot never to climb another volcano. We walked around slowly for a while, and every now and then one of the guides would get down on his hands and knees and check the ground for a trail. The trail was hard enough to see in broad daylight, but by now it was so dark it was almost impossible. By this time, even Mommy and Daddy were beginning to look a little nervous. After about twenty minutes of wandering around on and off on the trail, we came upon a house, where the guides each got a bottle torch — a beer bottle filled with kerosene, with an old rag sticking out as a wick. I wondered if Mommy and Daddy would let me make a torch like that; probably not a chance. The guides were now able to keep us on the trail, much to my relief.

We made it back to the truck and all piled in, exhausted. We were driven back to our car, said our good-byes, paid the guides, and headed home. I don't remember much after that because I fell asleep, I think, as soon as I hit the seat. Twelve and a half hours of hard, scary hiking had done me in.

I must say that for a while I was not thrilled when someone mentioned hiking volcanoes. I felt like I had been on a life-and-death climb and wasn't sure I ever wanted to do it again. Now as time has passed and I look back on it, I'm glad I went. I found out later that I was the youngest American ever to climb the mountain. I don't know if any Filipino boys my age have ever done it. The climb gave me a feeling of pride and accomplishment and in retrospect became one of the highlights for me of my time in the Philippines as a young Peace Corps Volunteer.

Looking for land leeches on the hot, wet climb.

Nancy, Caesar, and his sister

Oh No!
Another Move!

NANCY - 1972

Daddy's job was not working out. Even though he knew that it was the wealthy farmers who could most afford to implement better feeding programs for their piggeries and that these were the people the Bureau of Animal Industry wanted him to work with, he didn't like it. He felt that as a Peace Corps Volunteer he should be working with the poorer farmers, who needed help the most.

Peter and I weren't happy either. We didn't like our schools. I mean we really didn't like them, to the point where we felt we really couldn't deal with our unhappiness. The Catholic schools we attended were extremely strict, with a strong religious emphasis. They expected strict conformity with their rules, taught us by rote and memorization, and imposed harsh discipline. All this, combined with the total lack of encouragement of creative thinking, and the long school days with little physical activity, made the school very hard on us. Daniel was on a swim team at his school, and they weren't as strict with him. He thought it might have been because he was an American, so he did better at first. But even he got worn down by the constant conformity and boredom and did not want to go back another year. He also missed being in a co-ed school. Matthew was okay. Living in the States was fading fast in his three-year-old mind, and he didn't have to go to the schools.

We were all having problems with homesickness. We missed cool weather and our grandparents. I was ready to go home and go back to a farm, and so was Peter. Daddy even started looking into jobs back home. My parents wondered what they should do. Daniel's feelings were more mixed. No surprise to me, since sometimes he got to fly around in planes with Daddy being the oldest and a boy! No fair!

Daniel loved flying, getting a bird's eye view of the beautiful islands. From up in the air, the sprawling slums were usually not so visible. But on one trip, when Peace Corps flew us all to another island for our six-month medical checkups and more shots, we could see the solid miles of slums along some of the rivers and bays. They made a drab mosaic of seemingly overlapping rooftop after rusty rooftop, with a bit of green showing through now and then. In places the rooftops even seemed to flow into the water. It was an incredible sight. I imagine that is what Delia's community looked like from the air.

Our unhappiness was especially hard on Mommy. In addition to having to deal with all of us, she was concerned about losing her job because the center, which was running out of money, was talking about cutting out the preschool program. In addition to everything else, Peter was constantly fighting the heat. He just didn't know how to slow down and was irritable, tired, and pesky.

So many good things had happened since we'd become volunteers and there were lots of things we liked about being in the Philippines. Mommy felt if we could somehow get over what she called our "grrrr growl hump" we would be okay finishing out our stay. Daddy agreed, but he still thought about returning to the States if we couldn't work something out. We had barely been here a year since we started training back in July 1971, and we felt like we were on a sinking boat. Mommy always took a brighter view. She called these periods in our lives the thunderstorm periods, reminding us that the sun would shine again.

Finally my parents decided that if Peace Corps could relocate us to an area where we would have more school choices and Daddy could find a job he liked, we would stay. If not, we would return home to the United States. Mommy and Daddy really didn't want to leave because they believed so strongly in Peace Corps' work, but they had to think about us first. They met with the director of Peace Corps Volunteers in the Philippines about our schools and learned that the schools were a problem for some of the other families too, that one family had already returned to the States, and that being homesick was not unusual. Lucky for all of us, Peace Corps wanted to keep us too. They said if we could find jobs and schools in another area, they would let us move and stay.

The end of March was vacation time for our family, so that was when we went to check out other places to live. Our director had suggested Baguio, on the island of Luzon, as a possible place, because there were job possibilities and more choices in schools. It was in the mountains, where there were lots of trees and it was much cooler. It was also much more cosmopolitan. It was a favorite vacation place for Filipinos and foreign tourists, the U.S. had the John Hay Navel Base there, and it was where President Marcos went for vacations. We would not be the only strangers.

So off to Baguio we went. The mountains were fantastic in their ruggedness. There was nothing gradual or curving about them. The peaks were steep and rough, and the mountainsides full of gullies. The weather was a great improvement — in some ways it was like living in a Vermont summer all year round.

Daddy did find a job. He was hired to teach animal husbandry for a semester at Mountain State Agriculture College in the village of La Trinidad, which was located in the crater of a dormant volcano. He was comfortable with the job because most of the students came from poor rural families. And there were schools that seemed as though they would work well for us. We were ready to move. We were all sick of the hot, sweltering lowlands. Our homesickness faded away and we were ready for more adventures and getting to know this part of the Philippines.

But moving again meant having giving up our pets and having to start over again. One really good thing was that Delia was coming with us. My parents wanted her to see another part of her country, and it would save Mommy from having to find another maid. Delia was excited and so were my brothers and I: she was part of the family. Her move was a big deal in her community. Weeks before we left, friends came to say goodbye, and we had to assure her family that she could come home if she was unhappy.

We were pretty cross about having to give up our dog—who had just had puppies — my pet hen, our two cats, pig, and ducks. Daddy tried to figure out a way to take some of them, but finally decided that getting all of us to Baguio with all our luggage would be challenging enough. He built a big 4'x4'x8' wooden box to ship our household goods to Baguio. That box went on the boat with us and then from Manila to Baguio by truck. Caesar was very sad that we were leaving, but he hoped to visit us in Baguio. Hardest of all was saying good bye to the friends we had made. But we sure wouldn't miss the schools or the heat.

On June 4, 1972, we were on a boat back to Manila. Again we would be on the boat overnight, but this time not in a private cabin. We had to sleep in the dorms with the other passengers: the women, girls, and little children were in one large dorm, and the men and older boys in another. There were bunk beds with little room between them, and it was crowded, with no privacy. There was one bathroom for each dorm. We had become used to being the only whites among Filipinos and being stared and laughed at, but these Filipinos weren't used to an American family sleeping in their midst. All eyes were on us. And the staring, whispering, and giggling started. At first we were more comfortable than they were about us being there. But after a while, as we all went about the business of getting our little space in order, everybody relaxed and we were accepted.

I'll let Daddy tell about the rest of the journey.

"Once in Manila, we hired two jeepneys to haul us and our belongings to the Interboard Guest House. This was where we had stayed the night before we'd gone to Bacolod City. It was run by the Methodists, mostly for missionaries and the occasional Peace Corps Volunteers. Our room was hot, with only three uncomfortable beds that we had to share. The next morning we were up early and had to get all the way across Manila to the bus terminal, in time to get a 7:00 a.m. "express" bus. Now maybe you can understand why I decided not to haul a cat, dog, and chicken with us.

"Next we had to fight for seats on the bus. There was no way to buy tickets ahead of time and, as far as our experience had taught us, no one in the Philippines had ever heard of waiting in line. I shouted to Daniel to climb in a window at the back and pushed Frances, who was hanging onto Peter and Nancy, through the crowd of pushing, shoving people, as I clung to Matthew. As we fought our way forward, I struggled to keep sight of my family and saw Daniel disappear into the bus. While I had hoped we could sit near the front of the bus, we ended up all the way in the back, on seats that were 15 or 20 feet behind the rear axle. It meant every time the rear tire hit anything in the road, even a pebble, we would hit the ceiling. The kids didn't mind, but it was pretty hard on ducks and Daddies — and Mommies. Did I say ducks? Oh yes, I forgot to mention all the animals and luggage packed under and on top of the bus. And the bus itself was an ancient rattling old school bus like the one I rode to Dolly Madison School in Arlington, Virginia a very long time ago. We were in for a rough ride.

"The bus was hot and crowded, with people sitting on the arm rails and baggage stuffed everywhere. We had to bring our own food and water, for none of it was safe anywhere along the road. We were prepared for upset stomachs, not necessarily ours, and wiggly kids, including ours. And of course the quacking ducks, squealing pigs. And who knew what unforeseen disasters, like breaking down, awaited us. It took a slow seven hours, hitting the potholes in the paved straight road of the lowlands, and then twisting and bumping along the steep and narrow road up the mountain, to finally arrive in Baguio. Then we had to squeeze ourselves and our belongings into two jeepneys for the final leg to our new home. Once there, everybody breathed a huge sigh of relief. You know, these bus rides are good practice for building patience."

The house we rented in Baguio had two floors and was much bigger than the house we had had before, which had been too small for our family. We each, including Delia, had our own bedroom. The downstairs was all open, with the kitchen at one end. It had lots of windows, which made it very light inside. Mommy loved that, but not the flies that also came to live with us, since there weren't any screens. There was no heat in the house, so it got pretty chilly on cool nights and rainy days. What a change from the lowlands where we had never needed any heat! There was one bathroom, with a toilet and shower. There wasn't much in the house and we didn't have much to put in it but it was great having so much room, especially since Delia had come with us. And we never knew when Caesar would suddenly pop up to visit for a week, which he did—several times.

It wasn't long before Mommy had the house feeling like home, as she added the plants, Filipino art, our drawings, and hand carved wooden statues. Our favorite carving was of the carabao that we had all grown to love; and we had several, all different sizes. We lived in a small, quiet neighborhood on top of a hill that was surrounded by other hills and pine trees. Our house, along with five others, was set off the road in a cul-de-sac. The caretaker of our house lived in one of them and two were for sale. There were no fences around the houses and no guard dogs. We were high up enough in the mountains that often the clouds would come down and float among the hills, sometimes surrounding our house like a piece of soft veil flowing in and around us. The weather was delicious and cool enough so that sitting out in the sun was now a real pleasure. We quickly fell in love with our new home.

Our house also became a place for other visitors, including other Peace Corps Volunteers who came to Baguio for a vacation. And little groups of Daddy's students came over now and then to chat with Daddy and meet us.

In September our family got bigger, because for three weeks we had a ten-month-old baby move in with us. Her name was Marasi. Her parents—also Peace Corps Volunteers—were in the hospital with hepatitis and needed someone to care for their little girl. For a week she stayed overnight and then, for the last two weeks, she spent days with us and went home at night. We loved playing with her and helping take care of her, and she quickly got used to us. Matthew grew especially fond of her. Mommy learned how to carry Marasi on her back or side, attaching her, Filipino style, with a cloth that was a little smaller than a sheet. A few times she went to Baguio with the four of us with Marasi on her back and, you could tell by their smiles that it delighted the Filipinos who saw us.

Right after Marasi left, Vicky, a 20-year-old Filipino college student, came to live with us. Her family consisted of her mother and six brothers and sisters who were living in extreme poverty, with only rice to eat most of the time. Vicky was a good student, her English was good, and it was important for her to be able to finish her studies. Daddy had heard about her at the college he worked at, and we offered her room and board and her transportation to college. In return, she helped Delia with the housework. Mommy had quite a hard time convincing Vicky that she was not expected to carry a big part of the housework, because her studies were to come first. Vicky and Delia shared a bedroom, which delighted both of them. Delia had a new friend and Vicky had only one person to share a room with. We were now a family of eight. Good thing we had a big house!

Our life in Baguio really did change. In some ways it was almost as if we had moved to another country. Even the language changed. Delia couldn't understand it and had to fall back on the national language, Tagalog. This didn't work too well because in the Philippines most people used their own dialect rather than the national language. Thank goodness a lot of people spoke English.

It looked like our stay in Baguio would be a big success. We were ready to tackle our final year and finish out our assignment as Peace Corps Volunteers.

Our house in Baguio

Paul's shop students proudly show off the wooden toys they made

A Dream Job

FRANCES – 1972

I walked up the hill to the Good Shepherd's Convent in Baguio, preparing myself for my first meeting with Sister Helena. It was July and the campus was beautiful, with trees and well- trimmed lawns — very quiet and peaceful, not at all like most of the Philippines I had seen so far. Things had really changed since we'd moved from Bacolod City to Baguio. Daniel, Nancy, Peter, and even Matthew were now in schools that they liked. Paul had his job teaching at the Mountain State Agricultural College, and in a few months he was also going to work with Sister Helena to set up a carpentry program for out-of-school teenage boys who could not find work. The products would be wooden, heavy-duty playthings: blocks, trucks, rocking horses, etc. Sister Helena had assured him that she would be able to find a replacement for him when he left. We were so fortunate to have been able to move to Baguio and to have things fall into place so well for us, so we could complete our Peace Corps term.

For me, the prospect of working at the convent was exciting. Sister Helena, who had come from China many years before, met me with a big smile and open arms. Her English was excellent, which was a huge relief to me, as the language I had attempted to learn during training was not even spoken here. (There were so many different languages in the Philippines that it was hard even for Filipinos to understand each other.) She couldn't wait to tell me about what she wanted me to do: start a preschool program for three- to-six-year-olds. Right away I was caught up in her enthusiasm and felt that she and

I would do well together. As she showed me around the building where the school would be housed her excitement bubbled over. She said that while there were as yet no kids enrolled, she did not think that would be a problem. She explained that the families of the children lived in extreme poverty, in conditions similar to what we had seen in Bacolod City, and that without school many of the children would become beggars, even at their early age. She wanted something more for them. She did admit, however, that the key to winning the parents over would be my ability to gain their trust. Most of them had had little experience with foreigners, and I would be in charge—teaching and making decisions about the program without the input of other Filipinos. They might be resistant, at least at first, to putting their children under my care. She also hoped to hire a student teacher to work with me and take my place when I left. It was good to think of the school continuing. Continuity was not a given with Peace Corps and other social projects.

I told Sister Helena that I was concerned about the language barrier. I didn't speak their dialect, and the children didn't understand English. How would I communicate with them? She laughed and said that because the children spoke different dialects, they often didn't understand each other! So I was not to worry. That was easy for her to say, as I wondered how I would bridge the communication gap. Thank goodness Sister Helena was fluent in English.

We stepped into the room I would be teaching in. It had absolutely nothing in it. It didn't even have windows. But Sister Helena was undaunted. Her idea was for me to start from scratch. I was to decide everything, including what furniture I would need. She told me to let her know what I needed and she would get it. It took me a few minutes to take all this in. I was to start from scratch, furnish a classroom, develop a program, teach—while trying to figure out how to communicate with my students — train the student aide, and build up trust and confidence with my students and their parents. That was quite a challenge!

But I did it. I developed the preschool. Paul helped with making tables and wooden blocks, the John Hays Naval Base, located nearby, donated equipment for outdoor play, and Sister Helena and I figured out what the convent could afford in the way of supplies. I also used some of my children's books and magazines, which I hoped would begin to open my pupils' world a little bit. I was very pleased with the classroom when it was finished. It was pretty bare, compared to a preschool in the United States, but with the imagination and creativity I hoped to inspire in the children, I was sure we would have a grand time. Not only would they learn from me, I had a great deal to learn from them.

At the end of August I got the preschool off to a sporadic start. We had been having lots of rain, and since schools often closed in such bad weather, the first day of school was postponed twice. We had barely started, at last, when there were more days off due to rain, and we closed down for a week in September, when martial law was declared. When we did open the children — all 24 of them — and I were very excited, but the room was suddenly quite small, and I wondered how I would be able to work with so many, since I didn't have an aide yet.

Communication was difficult. The children were shy and very curious about me, and it took some time before they decided if they would stay or not. Every time I said anything, giggles would ripple through the room. On the first day, most of the boys ran away after about an hour and a half. This happened on a pretty regular basis for about a month, and I never knew how many children would show up. This, however, solved the problem of working with 24 children. I wondered if I was doing something wrong, but Sister Helena assured me that they would probably be back the next day. Some of them were, but only to leave again. By the end of the month, the children had settled in and my class size remained about 18, with a few who kept coming and leaving. I found it hard to adjust to this indifference in the children's schooling in this country where the need was so great. But after a while I just let it go.

I soon learned to communicate by doing. When I sat, they sat. When I first gave them paper and crayons, they just stared at them. I then drew a house on the blackboard and they got the idea. But they thought they were supposed to copy my drawing. It took some doing to help them see that they could draw whatever they wanted, and it didn't have to look like what I drew. And so it went until the student teacher arrived. With her understanding of simple English and her ability to translate, communication became easier. But it still wasn't perfect, since some of the children could not understand her either.

One day, on a walk, the children were running too far ahead. Without thinking, I called "Stop!" They just kept running.

I called again: "*Para, para!*" which I thought meant "Stop, stop!" The children stopped and stared at me and then started laughing. "*Para*" didn't mean stop in any of their languages. I never did learn what it meant. We soon sorted out what I wanted them to do, however, and from then on "*para, para*" became our word for stop. It always made them laugh.

Soon the children began to respond to me and we started having fun as we learned. I say "we" because I was learning also. Like all young kids, they loved to sing and dance. They loved it when I sang a simple good morning song, and said their names as I shook their hands. They loved to listen to me play the recorder. They loved art and the freedom to draw or color their own pictures the way they wanted to. It took a while for my aide to adjust to this; she had been taught that everybody did things exactly the way the teacher did. With Sister Helena's backing, I was able to help her understand how important it was for the children to think and create for themselves, how it would help them develop as individuals who could think independently and have new ideas.

The children loved it when we looked at books and magazines together, and this became a special time for us. They often laughed at me, because I couldn't speak their language, and laughed with me as we learned ways to communicate with each other.

Daniel, Nancy, Peter, and Matthew helped out whenever they had a chance. One day Peter helped the children learn how to play with blocks. They had no idea what to do with them. Here were 100 blocks that Paul had made and all they did was haul them around the room in the wooden trucks Paul and Daniel had also built. Usually I let children figure out for themselves what to do with things, but it soon it became obvious they hadn't a clue what to do here. So, I suggested to Peter that he show them other ways to use the blocks. He built a house. The watched, pointing and laughing as usual, but soon some of them were helping. It was a start. It was hard for a while for them to create new things by themselves, because they were used to copying something already made, but eventually they began to enjoy using the blocks to create their own structures.

Most of the children came to school barefoot, although a few wore flip-flops. The twin boys always wore red pullover sweaters. Another boy wore the same yellow sweater day after day. Some children wore hand-me-downs that were too big, and some wore outfits that were so old you couldn't help but wonder what kept them in one piece. But what they wore was always clean. Generally the kids looked happy, but many were extremely shy and wary. They spent a lot of time watching. You could tell they didn't get enough to eat, that their diet was mostly rice. Some probably had parasites, such as roundworms or tapeworms. Many of them were listless. Some came to school sick. Some got sick in my classroom, but we did not send them home. We just took care of them the best we could. It was hard to think about this and hard not to.

I began to understand how important my simple program of books, music, art, free play, and walks was to the children and even their parents, who were pleased to see their children happy at school and greatly appreciated the respect I showed both their children and them. I did not make them feel ashamed, and that was a really big deal in the Philippines. I was opening doors for the children. I offered them a freedom they had never known — the freedom to use their minds and figure out for themselves how they wanted to do something. For a little while, I also offered them control, consistency, and an acceptance that many had never known. They gained self-respect and respect for each other. Just as important, my student teacher was beginning to understand what I was trying to do within the framework of their way of life and was willing to continue in that vein after I left.

I knew I had made it with my students, of whom I was growing very fond, when one morning one of the little girls met me at the foot of the driveway, took my hand, and walked with me to class. I had gained their trust, they had accepted me. Here I was with anywhere from 10 to 20 little ones in a foreign country and feeling right at home. It made me remember what Nancy said so often: we were the same even though we were different.

We sing and dance, and around we go.

At the Buddhist temple we visited.

School Days

DANIEL – 1972 - 1973

School was never a big deal to me. I was lazy as a student, hardly ever using my brain to its full potential, according to all my teachers. My parents heard that constantly, even in the Philippines. I didn't like homework, didn't do it any more than absolutely necessary, and didn't study hard for tests, figuring if I hadn't learned it in class there wasn't any need to cram it in at the last minute. My sister just shook her head at me, having a keen interest in school and her studies; she didn't have time to spend fussing about my lack of interest in school in a family that thought highly of education and its importance. I knew it was important to get a good education, which is one reason I was keen on Peace Corps. Not only was it an adventure, it was an educational experience. I was excited about going to school in the Philippines, but it wasn't long before I was bored and restless at the school in Bacolod City. By the end of the year I was not a happy student and informed my parents that I didn't want to go back for another year.

Other Peace Corps families were also experiencing some of the same difficulties with schooling, so my parent knew they weren't being unreasonable in their concerns. We were lucky that we had the opportunity to move to Baguio and enroll in schools that were not based on the Filipino system, but were more like private boarding schools in our country. While Nancy told you about Chefoo School in Baguio, where she and Peter went, she left out a few things that I think are of interest and didn't say anything about Matthew's school or mine. We all had good experiences in Baguio, making us feel better about what we were doing there and even prompting us to consider staying another year. Just goes to show what a difference a good school can make.

Matthew went to a Montessori day school, run by Filipinos who believed in individual learning and a lot of hands-on activities for preschoolers. Matthew also went with Mommy to her preschool. Being a student in both places seemed to work well for him. Chefoo School, where Nancy and Peter went, was a very small missionary boarding school, with fewer than 20 students. Because it was so small, it was divided into two groups: grades 1, 2, 3–where Peter was in first grade, and 4, 5, 6–where Nancy was in fourth. The parents of most of the students were missionaries. There were no Filipinos in the school. The kids came from a variety of countries, as did the teachers. My school, Brent International School, had Filipino students as well as some from other countries. It was also a boarding school, for grades 1-12, and was much bigger than Chefoo. Both schools took a few day students from Baguio, which is why we were able to go.

Our schools, including those where our parents were working, all started and ended the school year at different times. Vacations, holidays, and rain days were also often not the same. We all had Christmas off, but the length of the time off differed. Nancy and Peter's school was year-round. They went to school for three months, were off for five weeks, back to school for three months, and so on. When we got to Baguio in June their school had been in session since May, so they started right away. My school, however, had a more traditional nine-month schedule: it didn't start until August and finished in May. Matthew's school started in July, and Daddy started teaching at his college in the beginning of July. Matthew had a lot of days off for rain. Mommy finally got her school running in August and also had a lot of rainy day holidays. Sometimes Mommy had a hard time remembering who was going off to school and who was staying home, but we managed.

Nancy and Peter walked up the hill to their school. I took a jeepney with a group of Brent day students at 7:15 in the morning and arrived back home about 3:30. I also had homework, which I did not like. Matthew also rode a jeepney to his school. On his first day Mommy went with him and he cried when she left, but he said he had cried for only a little bit and that the next day he was going to ride the blue jeepney without her. He did and was very proud.

Brent looked like a small college campus. I was in the 7th grade. My classes, all with no more than 16 students, were held in different buildings, and I really liked that. I had five minutes between classes, a 30-minute lunch break, and a 15-minute recess. One of my classes was actually a club and my choice was to join the Boy Scouts. In addition our classes, we also had work projects. One of mine was helping to build terraces for flowers on the hillside. I also enjoyed building a radio and an intercom in science. They both worked!

While our schools were very strict, they were also relaxed and quite informal at times. They encouraged individuality and creativity, learning how to work within a group and to become good citizens. Nancy mentioned sitting around a fireplace in her school, and we did the same at Brent. Classes were sometimes outside under the shade of a tree and in our classrooms we did not always have to sit quietly at our desks. We could sit or lie around the room for some of our activities. Both schools had a lot of hands-on projects as well as written and oral reports. Peter loved working with clay and getting his hands messy. He helped make puppets out of papier mache for a puppet show his class put on. He also played the big goat in "The Three Billy Goats Gruff," Baby Bear in "Goldilocks and the Three Bears," and the narrator in the "Three Little Pigs." Peter had come a long way since we'd started in Peace Corps. Nancy and her group wrote and performed a Thanksgiving play. She played the Pilgrim mother and enjoyed that very much.

Our last days of school were all different too. Nancy and Peter were in school right up until we left the Philippines, at the end of June 1973. I ended my school year the middle of May. Matthew's school ended the middle of April, and he went to a summer session in May. At the end of May he also took part in Mommy's end-of-year program with her students. He played a horse in a skit about Humpty Dumpty. That program was a big event for Mommy. We would soon be returning to the States and they had a going away party for her. Daddy worked with his shop students as much as he could, right up until near time for us to leave. Now if you think all of that is confusing, I have not included Vicky and her schedule, which was too complicated to describe. Somehow it all worked out and we had a very good year, even though the teachers complained about me not reaching my potential and I didn't get any credit for Spanish, because I had such a low grade.

Nancy, Peter, and I enjoyed going with Mommy to her preschool. She always put us to work. It gave us a chance to share with and learn from her students. I enjoyed most going with Daddy when he started the carpentry shop at the Good Shepherd Convent. After my school year was over I spent a great deal of time with him there. Again I got the chance to help and learn. Being a part of our parents' work enabled Nancy and me to understand what being an adult Peace Corps Volunteer was all about. That was an education in itself.

There was another part of our education that my parents felt was very important. While we were living and working among the poor, they wanted us to know of the beauty that also existed. This included cultural activities. Nancy and Daddy went on a trip to Manila so Nancy could get some new glasses. They stayed overnight and he took her to see *My Fair Lady* at the performing arts center. Another time all of us went there to see professional dancers in beautiful costumes perform Filipino dances, including the Tinikling, which I've already told you about.

The beginning of December 1972, Peace Corps required us and the other volunteers who had trained with us to go to Cebu City for nine days for medical checkups and progress check-ins. We also used the time for a mini-vacation. Cebu City is on an island east of Negros Occidental, where we had lived in Bacolod City, and was also very hot. This travel, which Peace Corps paid for, was different from our usual trips. We went to Manila on a public express bus that required reserved tickets, which meant not fighting the crowds—definitely a new experience. From there we flew to Cebu City and I had a glimpse of Mount Canlaon. It was hard to believe I had climbed it.

Once there, we were checked from head to toe, including our eyes and teeth, and we had stool, blood, and urine tests. At the end of three days of doctor visits our family and the other volunteers were invited to dinner with the U.S. Consul and his wife, Dan and Margaret Sullivan. They knew Grandma and Grandpa Stone very well and had even voted for Grandma when she was elected to the House of Delegates in Virginia. I couldn't believe it! Here I was half way around the world and I was being introduced to somebody who knew my grandparents. As a result, they invited us to spend the day at a private beach with some Filipino friends, who had four children around our ages. We were so excited that we were finally going to go to a clean beach with clean clear blue water. We had a great time playing in the ocean and being a part of this upscale Filipino family, who didn't see us as different.

We also visited a large Chinese Buddhist temple on a hill overlooking the city and the ocean. It was covered with colored lights that were turned on at night. It was awesome. The statues of dragons, roosters, lion-like creatures, and the wall paintings with lots of birds and flowers were amazingly beautiful. The temple was made up of several buildings connected by covered walkways and courtyards. The biggest was the one for worship: a lovely quiet room with no pews, just a big floor to sit on and meditate and in the front was the beautiful altar. Before entering it you took off your shoes. The whole place was very quiet and peaceful.

While in Cebu City, we also went to a revolving restaurant on top of one of the tallest buildings. It was quite a sensation, sitting up there surrounded by glass and seeing the city below us, as the restaurant slowly turned. During dinner a band and singers provided background music. One of the musicians went from table to table asking for requests and they played "Oh Susanna" and "Yankee Doodle" for us. The other diners got a big kick out of that, as did we. All of this to help us see that there was more than poverty in the country, there was also great beauty, culture, and innovation. But our enjoyment of all these was still shadowed by the knowledge that they were available to only a very few, while so many had so little, were often hungry, and in many cases were barely housed.

Our education in the Philippines did not come from just our schools in Bacolod City and Baguio. The whole country and its people – the poor and wealthy – were our classrooms and, our teachers.

A fun day at the ocean in Cebu City

Hats to keep off the sun and rain

And The Rain Came Down

You can't imagine what a rainy season is like until you have lived in the Philippines and a typhoon comes blowing in and hangs around for 30 straight days. It rained hard most of the time for 21 days, and we didn't see the sun at all. After that we saw the sun for a little bit each day, and the rain did not come down as hard, but it still rained. Daddy said we'd had more than two hundred inches of rain since he'd started keeping track of it on July 6th. That's about eight inches a day. It felt like it would never stop. Peter and I were the only ones going to school at the time. Matthew's and Mommy's schools had closed because of the rain, and Daniel's hadn't started yet. A few times, when the rain and wind were really bad, Mommy got us a ride with a neighbor. Most days Peter and I sloshed up the hill to our school, well protected from the cold and wet. As we passed the little cluster of makeshift tin homes, I wondered how the squatters living there survived this chilly rain. Mommy said that the cold was one of the reasons some babies and small children got sick and died. I worried about them.

Because we had no inside heat, our house was very damp and chilly. We had to wear long pants and shirts and sweaters to stay warm. When we went to bed, the sheets and blankets were damp and cold. Our mattresses were damp and, worse, they smelled bad because they were stuffed with old rags and some kind of plant. Our walls, which were already covered with fly spots, became mildewed and turned a dark color. My bedroom not only had mildewed walls, there were also droplets of water clinging to my ceiling. I kept waiting for one to drop, which it didn't, thank goodness! Mommy, Daddy, and Delia had to keep scrubbing the walls to get rid of the mildew. Mommy always tried to stay positive. The mildew helped dampen the fly spots so she could really get the walls cleaned, she insisted. I must admit after they scrubbed my bedroom walls, they looked like they were freshly painted.

Nothing was safe from mildew. Daddy left a pair of pants hanging on his bedroom door for two days, and when he went to put them on they were covered with gray mold. One week, a couple of pairs of blue jeans got a very bad sour smell, because after three days they still hadn't dried. Our books got moldy, and we had to cram them close together so they would not warp. Even the floors got moldy. Mommy wondered if battling the mold was worth it.

"Sometimes I think I should just forget about it until the sun comes out, but I'm afraid if I do, the house would get so bad that even we would start getting moldy," she said. That gave us a little something to laugh about.

Not all the water went to waste. We caught rainwater from the roof in large buckets and dumped it into the army water tank we kept, because the city water had been turned off. The rainwater was actually cleaner than the water we got from the town. Mommy boiled our drinking water for 30 minutes before she would let us drink it. We all had to help carry water for everything: cooking, flushing the toilet, washing clothes, and bathing. Hard work! Once during the rain the drain system into our house plugged up, and for two days we had to go to the toilet in a bucket and bury the contents outside. All the other used water had to be hauled back outside and dumped on the ground. Then the electricity went off for short periods of time for two days. I longed for sunny days.

It was hard work getting our clothes washed and dried. Mommy started leaving the two burners of the stove on for part of the day to help get some of the dampness out of the house and help dry the clothes. Even dry, they still felt damp and clingy when we put them on. Mom developed a system for laundry that she will tell you about.

"It took a while but I finally developed a system to get clothing washed and dried. It was a headache, but I got used to it. Each evening after supper I picked out things to be washed, taking into account what we needed, how long it would take them to dry, how much room there was to hang them. Then Delia and I put them into laundry tubs to soak overnight. In the morning, Delia washed them. That was the easy part. I removed clothes already hanging in the "drip room" – a small storage room off our kitchen – so Delia could hang the newly washed clothes there. I hung some of the heavier clothes – especially blue jeans – above the two gas burners to dry more quickly. Some of the clothes we put on a special line hung up in Nancy's room, where they dried slowly – very slowly. Some went on a line in the upstairs hall to dry a bit faster. Things that were almost dry went onto a line in Delia's room. But nothing actually got dry; everything was still damp. During the day I moved the clothes around. Those over the stove became ready for ironing. Those in Nancy's room went either to hang above the stove or out in the hall. Some of the ones in the hall never made it to Delia's room because they got dry enough there to iron. This went on day after day – lots of laundry, lots of ironing. But after a while it became routine.

"Bed linens were a different problem. It took a week to get three sheets dry. We didn't have room to hang up any more than that. I was having a hard time keeping up. Then I got lucky. Nancy and Peter must have said something about our laundry problems to the woman who sometimes drove them to school. When she found out we had no heat, no hot water, no washer or dryer, she took my linens home to dry for two weeks. What a lifesaver! But I sure was glad when the rain stopped."

We did manage to have fun, despite the rain. We went outside and splashed and waded in the water that was everywhere. And some days the whole family went for walks. Indoors we worked on a braided rug made out of rags. Mommy gave me a cardboard box that I covered with colored paper to make a bed for my doll. One of the bedrooms had a balcony over the living room, and Daddy hooked up a rope and pulley and let Daniel and Peter haul things up and down on it. They pulled their bikes up and even tried to pull themselves up. That didn't work! I had some turns too. We had books to read, pictures to draw and color, games to play, and the braided rug kept getting bigger and bigger. Mommy gave us exercises to do, including running laps around the living room. We were all right.

Our garden rotted away in all that rain. But much worse happened to other people: water loosened the sides of the steep hills around us, and mudslides began. In one seven houses were destroyed and people were killed or injured. Mommy's dressmaker lived right next to one of the mudslides. She was safe but had to move out of her house. Daddy and Daniel spent a couple of days trying to help the people affected. There wasn't a whole lot they could do, but they did get a close look at the destruction. Our house was well protected from the slides and the trees around it kept us from being able to see them, but when we took the jeepney into town, we could see the mudslides and the damage. One jeepney driver knew one of the people killed. He said that after it was over, people were going to be hungry and angry, that that would cause a civil war.

Before the rains came Mommy had bought extra food, so we were not hungry. The main road to the lowlands and Manila was washed out, and hardly anything was coming up to Baguio. It took three days rather than six hours to get supplies up to Baguio. For a while nobody from the lowlands could get to Baguio at all, because the airport and all the roads were closed.

From the newspaper we learned about all the flooding in the lowlands. Bridges and roads were washed out. Towns and farmlands were flooded, and many homes and other buildings were underwater. Thousands and thousands of people had to leave their homes. It seemed like all of Luzon Island was underwater, and the mountains and Baguio were an island all by themselves. All the schools on the island closed, except Peter's and mine. Sometimes I worried about our house, but Daddy said that because we had grass all around us and the water running around us was clear, we were safe. Still it was awful — scary and exciting at the same time.

Just before the rains stopped in the middle of August, Peter and I started our five-week school vacation and Daniel started school. Now Mommy had Peter home all day, and because he was so active, she said she had to have nerves of steel. I think she really must have had them, because Peter was always on the go, except when he was sleeping. One day she just bundled him and Matthew up in rain gear and walked them to town to buy a few things. They loved it. They had a lot of uphill and downhill walking. They ran under all the leaking downspouts, waded through gushing runoff water that slopped over their boots, and dodged the crowds of umbrellas along the sidewalk. Rain or shine, Baguio still overflowed with people. Peter and Matthew bubbled over telling us about their adventure.

Finally, after what seemed like forever, the sun began to shine again. Suddenly there were mattresses and pillows outside everywhere, out in the sun to dry, even ours. What a relief and joy to go back to warm, sunny days!

One of many mudslides caused by all the rain

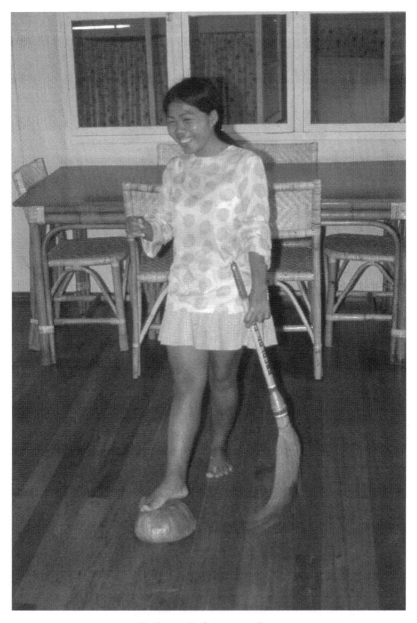

Delia polishing our floor

Martial Law and Christmas

DANIEL - SEPTEMBER 1972 - JANUARY 1973

One day in late September Delia came running into the house, almost in tears. She said she needed to lower the hems on all her skirts because the police were stopping girls on the street and slashing their skirts because they were too short. She'd seen it happen. Daddy, Nancy, and I hopped on a jeepney into Baguio City to see what was going on, leaving Peter and Matthew with Mommy. We didn't see any skirts being cut, but as we stood on the sidewalk and looked out into the street policemen were grabbing guys with long hair and cutting off a chunk of their hair. They were stopping buses and jeepneys and pulling guys off and cutting off chunks. They even went after some of the jeepney drivers. There was hair on the sidewalks and road. We heard that an American had been stopped and had his hair clipped as well as his beard. Nancy and I wondered what skirts and hair had to do with martial law.

President Marcos had declared martial law just a few days before, on September 21, 1972. This had not come as a surprise to our parents because there had been bombings, killings, and threats to President Marcos in the greater Manila area ever since we had moved to Baguio, in June. And the International Airport in Manila had been burned down. Our parents knew that hatred of President Marcos and his corrupt government was the main reason for the violence. His term as president was going to be over soon, and he was determined to remain in office, even though the constitution did not permit him to run again. Because of the political unrest and the danger to himself Marcos, with his army backing him up, declared martial law throughout the entire country. It gave him the power to make new laws and ignore old ones. It meant he could cancel the elections. President Marcos was very serious about all of this because he said he was going to build what he would call the "New Society" and make a new constitution for the people. But my parents said it was all so that he could stay in power. We soon learned just what martial law meant and the different ways it would affect us. I never understood about the hair and skirts except they seemed to have been considered signs of being radical.

One way martial law directly affected me was that I could no longer buy firecrackers. That was a real bummer as far as I was concerned, because I really liked setting them off. When martial law was declared, all the schools in the country were shut down – from nursery school all the way to college – and remained closed for at least a week. That wasn't what I called a hardship, but Mommy and Daddy hoped they wouldn't be closed for long, since it meant they couldn't go to work. There was also concern that if things got really bad under martial law, if there was increased violence or threats to Americans, all Peace Corps Volunteers would be sent home. Luckily it never got that bad.

One of the first things that happened was the setting of a curfew; everyone had to be off the streets and in their homes by seven o'clock in the evening and could not leave them until the next morning at six a.m. People who didn't obey could be arrested. After a week the hours changed to between midnight and four a.m. They would change again and again, and often, because communication was so poor, we had no idea what they were. To prevent political talk or violent action, people were not allowed to gather in groups or go to parties. Movie theaters, which usually stayed open seven days a week from morning until late at night, were closed down, as were nightclubs and gambling halls. Newspapers, magazines, TV and radio stations were shut down too. Reporters who didn't agree with the president and what he was doing were arrested. People were not allowed to travel or leave the country. Because anyone who disagreed with the president might be arrested, some people went into hiding. One of the safe places to go was the convent where Mommy worked. The nuns opposed President Marcos and protected the people who came to them for shelter.

After a week elementary schools reopened, but high schools and colleges remained closed. In October, some of the colleges opened, but only for third- and fourth-year students. When Daddy went back to work he found that his class sizes were smaller, because some of the students had gone into hiding or had been arrested – they simply disappeared. Most high schools were still closed, but mine got special permission to reopen. A few radio and TV stations and one newspaper that was owned by the president were allowed to broadcast and publish, but the news was censored. That meant that the government decided what news they would allow the people at home and abroad to hear. It also meant that we did not get any news from the United States.

In November President Marcos relaxed martial law a bit more, but there were still lots of rules about what you could and couldn't do. For instance, colleges were now open for all the students, but they had to wear a pass to get on campus. College newspapers were banned, as were extracurricular activities, and students had to be off campus by a certain time. One of the rules even applied to us. My parents had to sign a paper at the post office, allowing the film they mailed home to be opened for inspection. They didn't know why it was only for film and not for letters.

Movies, magazines, and books came under a different censorship from the newspapers and needed special approval to be printed or shown. Newspapers started publishing again, but since speaking against the government was not allowed, they all said pretty much the same thing.

One of the laws required people to turn in their weapons, and the newspapers published photos of huge piles of handguns and rifles. But we heard that for every weapon that was turned in, one was kept. I thought that turning in weapons was a good idea. In the Philippines, lots of people carried them. At some movie theaters they even had a sign up at the ticket booth that said "Place your firearms here." And many people carried knives that were much bigger than pocketknives. I never saw anybody being stabbed or shot, but it was something you heard about all the time, and sometimes I would see a gun sticking out of a man's pocket.

There was still a curfew, and many of the gambling places and nightclubs remained shut down. The one gambling activity that was allowed was cock-fighting, which was a really big deal in the Philippines. It was odd that while cockfights were permitted, there were restrictions on who could go to them. Teachers and civil servants – people who work for the government – were not allowed to go and if caught there would be fired. There were people who raised roosters just for this cruel and bloody sport. When we lived in Bacolod City, there was a flock of roosters being raised to fight just down the street. What happened in a cockfight was this: they put two roosters – sometimes with sharp little metal spurs on their legs – in a little arena and they fought each other with their beaks and legs until one was near death and a winner declared. Sometimes the roosters actually died, but this didn't happen often, because the roosters were valuable and their owners wanted them to live to fight another day. The spectators, who were mostly men, bet big money on the fights. Then there were informal cockfights. It was not unusual to see a group of men sitting in a circle on the street, watching two roosters go at it and betting on the result.

The curfew remained. One night Mommy and Daddy went out to get some ice cream – a rare treat that we hadn't had in Bacolod City – and were stopped by the police. They asked them who they were, where they were going, where they lived, and why they were out after curfew. Daddy said he didn't know it was past curfew time. They came home without ice cream, which didn't please us at all. Although being stopped by the police was a serious matter,

Daddy made a funny story out of it, to help keep us from worrying too much. Mommy and Daddy never seemed to keep straight when curfew was, because they were stopped another time and sent home.

One of the things that made us realize just what martial law meant happened at Christmas time. Our second Christmas was very different from the first. Firecrackers were still banned, so that meant it was a quiet Christmas and New Year. There were also no carolers or dancers. We did hear that there were a few carolers out, but they had to get a special permit, and they didn't come to our neighborhood. There were no Christmas parties, no big family gatherings. We did go to a church service on Christmas Eve and and Christmas Day. And we did get a tree. Well, sort of.

Baguio was high enough in the mountains and cool enough that some pine trees grew there. We had one in our yard. It was big enough for Daddy to put up a rope swing with a seat at the bottom, and there was almost always somebody on it. We couldn't cut down a tree, and most wouldn't have made very good Christmas trees anyway. Daddy came up with a solution, as one of our parents usually did: we would make a tree. We all stared at him and Mommy just shook her head. We went out with Daddy and cut branches from pine trees and brought them home. Daddy made a tree trunk out of a two- by-four, in which he drilled holes for the branches. Then, with our help, he stuck the branches in the holes and tied them so they would stay up. It was really funny-looking. But there was lots of space between the branches, and we hoped the decorations we made would improve its appearance. Vicky taught us how to make Christmas balls. We bought some green plastic balls — a little smaller than a tennis ball — and stuck straight pins decorated with designs of colorful beads and sequins into them, It took a long time to fill a ball with the decorated pins, but it was a lot of fun, and the balls were beautiful. The four of us didn't get that many made, but Vicky and Mommy pitched in, so we had a good supply for the tree. It didn't look half bad once it was all decorated. We were really proud of it.

The biggest gift for this second Christmas was that Grandma and Grandpa Stone came for a visit. They came around the middle of December and stayed until a week after New Year's. Daddy and Mommy had to figure out where they would stay when they were here, so Daddy wrote them:

"We think it is a good idea for you to stay in the hotel while here in Baguio, since there are eight of us living here now. Person number eight being Vicky, a college student, living very happily with us. Our bathroom is kind of small and all eight of us use it, and the clothes are washed in it, and the dog drinks in it, and the cat pees in it, and we all take baths in it, and I have to chase Delia — our maid — out every time I need to warm the king's throne, and I shave in it, and the kids brush their teeth in it, and we collect water in it, and the kids sometimes play in the water in it — in a wash pan not the toilet — and if that isn't enough, our pet frogs sleep in it. Well again I don't want to bias your decision, but our beds are lousy, we never have water, and as I said before our bathroom is a bit busy — there usually is a line up outside the door several people long, some holding on to their britches for dear life."

So Grandma and Grandpa didn't stay in our house but rented a cottage nearby instead. It was a much better-equipped house than ours, with hot water for showers and a stove with an oven. Grandma baked us two cakes and some brownies. I had forgotten how good a brownie tasted.

Once again Santa found us. Once again we did our Christmas morning. It was just extra special because of Grandma and Grandpa. They took us to Christmas dinner at the nearby John Hay U.S. Air Force Base, where we had a full course American-style turkey dinner. Grandma Stone couldn't imagine any other type of dinner at Christmas and of course we loved it. Grandpa and Daddy played miniature golf and we got to walk around the base without being followed or stared at. Being on the base also gave us a chance to see how differently Americans who were not Peace Corps Volunteers lived in this country. Military families stayed on the bases, other families lived in what we called "regular houses," with all the conveniences, and a maid who did the marketing, probably a gardener, maybe a laundress, and a car. We didn't see any other families living among the Filipinos the way we were. No wonder Filipinos thought we were rather odd.

Actually in Baguio, we were not followed, stared at, and pinched as much as we had been in Bacolod City. I think that was because Baguio attracted many foreign tourists. But even here a Peace Corps Volunteer family was still different. People might have seen "white" people and maybe individual Peace Corps Volunteers, but they had not seen a Peace Corps Volunteer family. Even Caesar, our parents' co-workers, and other friends, were having their first experience with one. It reminded me that each of us, as members of a Peace Corps family, had a role: to be people of good will.

Christmas had another surprise for us. I was at work with my mother one day when Sister Helena came in and told her to come and pick out a puppy before she went home. We were both rather puzzled, because nobody had been talking about a puppy for Christmas. We already had a skinny dog with gray hair called Shadow. I crossed my fingers behind my back and wondered what Mommy was going to say. She said okay and lucky me, I got to pick out the puppy. It was brown and white and part beagle. Sister Helena delivered it just before Christmas. Mommy said it was definitely a Santa puppy. Nancy, Peter, Matthew, and I were delighted. We named her Amiga, which is Spanish for "female friend." A male pup would have been called Amigo.

We were also invited by Sister Helena to have an American Christmas dinner at the Good Shepherd Convent. She was delighted to meet our grand-parents. So our second Christmas was much more American than our last but still different from that at home back in the States.

There was one sad event over Christmas: Delia decided she wanted to return home. It had been hard for her to make friends, mainly because of the language difference, and she had become homesick and unhappy. After she left – a few weeks before Christmas – Mommy decided not to get another maid. We would be there only six more months, and we figured that with

Vicky and the rest of us pitching in, we could handle the marketing, laundry, and housecleaning. We missed Delia as a friend, and Mommy missed her help with the house, but we all adjusted to helping out more.

On New Year's Day, we did get to go to a party, but it wasn't really a party as far as I was concerned. We were on a three-day trip into the mountains north of Baguio to visit the famous Banaue Rice Terraces with our grandparents and Vicky. We rented a big van – with driver – and rooms in a very modest hotel. The hotel had a New Year's party but, all they did was give speeches about the "New Society," voting for the new constitution, and being good citizens. And, believe it or not, they even talked about not getting drunk and having good manners. It was nothing like the parties we had been to the year before in Bacolod City. It was as though we were in a different country: because we were in a different place and because of martial law.

The rice terraces going up the steep mountainsides were almost beyond description. Their beauty and peaceful look were spectacular. They were like giant steps carved out of the mountain, some going up to an altitude of more than 4,000 feet. We were able to walk out on the terraces, whose walls were made of clay. We were walking on terraces that had been made by hand 2,000-3,000 years ago! Snuggled down among the terraces were small groups of two to four nipa huts that were the homes and farm centers of the farm families. One family invited us to have a close look at their home. Under the nipa hut that was high up in the air, and tucked in the corner under the floor next to one of the posts, was an unusual-looking package. Mommy being ever curious, and having an idea about what it was, found somebody who could understand enough English and asked about it. It held a few bones from their ancestors, kept there in memory of them and to keep their home safe. That was something really different and a new thing to learn about people and their beliefs.

We all felt a little lonely after Grandma and Grandpa left. They had seen our schools, met our friends, seen where Mommy and Daddy worked, and gone on several trips with us. I began to feel a little homesick for my own country, but I wasn't ready to leave just yet, even though we were still under martial law and I still couldn't buy firecrackers.

The Banaue Rice Terraces

Walking along the walls of the terraces

Christmas in Baguio.
The tree we made is in the corner.

Martial Law Was Scary

PETER - SEPTEMBER
1972 - 1973

I ran into the house calling my mother. She was there and I plunged right in. "In school today we had to pray. We had to pray that the bombings in Manila would stop. And they told us some people don't like President Marcos. Why don't they like him? Why are there bombings?"

Mommy replied, "Some people don't like President Marcos because they don't think he does enough to help his people, and some of the bombings are because they don't like him."

"Well, I don't like bombing." I said, as I ran out the door to play with Daniel and Shadow. I forgot all about the bombing.

Then something else happened that was hard for me to understand. President Marcos declared martial law. Mommy said we couldn't go to school because of it. That was fine with me at first, but after a few days I missed it. I really liked my school and the things we did. After a week Nancy and I could go to school again, but Daniel's school did not start again until October.

Then another thing happened. People started painting the rocks along the roads all white. They were painting all of them, big ones and little ones. Mommy said it was because under martial law, the people had to clean up the roads and their towns and their yards. But it still seemed funny to paint all those rocks; they weren't dirty.

A lot of time went by and we had Christmas, which wasn't as much fun with martial law forbidding parties, but Grandma and Grandpa came and we had a funny Christmas tree. For a little while I forgot about martial law. After Christmas, though, it started to worry me. I saw pictures of big piles of guns in the newspaper, and people were burning grass in their yards and on the hillsides. The burning made lots of smoke. Our neighbor burned his yard and we could smell the smoke in our house. Mommy explained that the guns were being collected so that there would not be so many in private hands. And that everybody was burning grass as a way to clean things up. I didn't really understand all this, and the fires were scary.

One day at school "Uncle" – the dorm father for boarding students – told us that if any Chefoo students were caught throwing paper on the ground, the police would arrest them and put them in jail for thirty days. "Uncle" said he knew a man already in jail for dropping paper in the park. Cleaning up had become a big issue under martial law. They even sent groups of school children out in the streets to help clean things up. I was careful not to throw paper on the ground, but I was still worried. I didn't want to go to jail and didn't want my friends to either.

One day the caretaker of our house, who lived nearby, went into our garden and dug up some of our plants. He wanted to mow the grass in our yard. He didn't think we were keeping it clean. Daddy talked to the caretaker and asked him not to do that again, reminding him that our yard was very clean, but I still worried about it. One day when nobody was looking, I went into our garden and started trying to clean it up. I didn't want the police to come and arrest us. When I went back into the house, Mommy asked why I was so dirty. I started to cry, "I was trying to clean the garden. The caretaker told me that the police were going to come and check our place to see if it was clean. I don't want to be arrested."

Mommy took me in her arms and said, "Peter, we are not going to be arrested. Remember when we first moved in here, we cleaned up our yard and the lot next door to us. We keep our yard clean. And that little dried-up tomato plant is still producing tomatoes, so it's okay for it to be there." I dried my tears, and Mommy said that she would tell Daddy to talk to the caretaker – again!

I also worried about the fires. One day I saw a group of little boys watching a fire not far from our house. I didn't see any adults around and the fire looked dangerous, so I tried to put it out. Soon some older boys came and told me to leave. I went home and again in tears, told Mommy about it. Later that day a boy came to our house and told my parents to tell me not to put the fires out.

Then the awful day came, the day I had so worried about: a policeman came to our house. Only Mommy was home. He told her that a neighbor had complained that we were not being helpful in cleaning up the neighborhood. He kept looking around the yard, trying to find something messy. Mommy told him that we had cleaned not only our yard but also the two lots next to us, but the policeman didn't seem convinced. When he spied our sandbox, he told Mommy to get rid of it. That didn't make sense. Matthew and I played there all the time. Even Daniel and Nancy did sometimes. Obviously he didn't know what a sandbox was! I guess he believed Mommy's explanation because he finally left, and we kept the sandbox. Mommy had saved the day!

She told Daddy about it at supper. The way she told it, I could even laugh a little about it and not be as worried. But our clean-up problems weren't over. After supper the caretaker set the lot next to us on fire. Daddy got angry. He and the caretaker had had this argument about burning the grass so many times. Daddy looked like he was going to explode and stomped out of the house. We could see him swinging his arms as he talked, but we couldn't hear what he was saying. When he finally came back in, he and the fire had cooled down.

The next day the caretaker came to our house and apologized for burning the lot next door. Then Daddy and he started talking about composting and how it worked. Before the caretaker left, Daddy gave him a little book about it. Daddy had not made the caretaker feel ashamed and we didn't have any more problems with him.

I sort of got use to martial law and wasn't as scared about it. Nothing bad ever happened to us because of it, but I didn't like it.

Dogs, Carabaos, and Other Animals

NANCY – 1971-1973

It was hard having pets while we were in Peace Corps. Filipinos didn't really have pets the way we do in the States, at least poor people didn't. There were lots of dogs, chickens, pigs, ducks, and carabaos. We also saw some cows and horses, but not many other kinds of animals. Most of the animals were used for food or as work animals. We saw lots of carabaos and thin horses pulling work carts. Carabaos were used in the rural areas for working in the fields and hauling goods. The horses were used a lot in transporting people, as we saw in the lowlands where they pulled the *calesas*. Some of the big cattle ranches had horses for working with the cattle. We didn't see many horses in Baguio, but there were lots of carabaos.

People with lots of money had guard dogs. Some used geese to guard their homes. We could hear the geese honking as we walked past the walls that surrounded the property, or sometimes a dog barking. Sometimes when we walked past a gate, dogs would run up to it, snarling and showing their teeth. They looked awfully mean, and they were. One evening Mommy went out for a walk along our road, and as she passed one of the walled-in homes, a dog suddenly dashed out through the open gate on the driveway, snarling and baring his teeth, and stopped right in front of her. Mommy froze and wondered what to do. She was sure that if she moved the least little bit, the dog would attack. There they were, dog and Mommy, frozen in place. After what seemed like a long time, though it was probably only a few minutes, a guard with a rifle in hand came down the driveway, took the dog back inside, and closed the gate. He never said a word to her. Mommy just stood there for a while, waiting for her heart to stop racing and her stomach to settle down, and headed back to the house. She couldn't believe how close she had come to being seriously hurt and that the guard hadn't even seemed concerned. Luckily that was our only encounter with a guard dog, but if that happened to Mommy who was just walking by, it must have happened to others when gates were carelessly left open. I hope they also managed to get away unhurt.

There were dogs everywhere that were not guard dogs; they hung around with people in their homes, at their work. Where there were people, there were dogs. I don't know if they were pets or not. They were skinny, full of fleas, and always looked hungry. Then there were stray dogs that had no home and just wandered about getting whatever scraps they could find. Rabies was often a problem among the dogs, and that is one of the reasons we got rabies shots when we became volunteers. Our plan was to leave dogs alone and not get bitten. Despite all of this, we ended up with our own dogs. When we lived in Bacolod City, the neighbor's dog, which was skinny and shy, crept through the rickety fence into our yard, where of course we fed her. She got friendlier and friendlier as we kept on giving her food, and after a while she made herself right at home and claimed us. We were delighted. It felt so good having a dog, even if she wasn't really our own. We called her Lady. The neighbors never complained. Maybe they figured it was a good way to get her fed. When we left Bacolod City, the neighbors took Lady back.

We had two dogs in Baguio, our second year. Amiga, the one we got at Christmas as a puppy, was very friendly and healthy. It really worried me that she might be stolen, probably to eat, so I made sure she was always safe. One day I watched a truck full of dogs in wire cages stacked up high drive by my house. I knew those dogs were going to be killed for food. As I watched, I held Amiga tight. We taught Amiga to sit, lie down, and stay, and Daniel, to earn one of his Boy Scout badges, taught her some tricks. We really loved her and it didn't seem fair that we had to leave her behind when we returned to the States. A friend of Daddy's who was a veterinarian took her and said he would not eat her. That helped me feel a little better.

Our other dog was Shadow. That was a good name for him because he was gray and very skinny. Shadow was a stray that found us and came with a million fleas. They were visible, crawling all over him. So the first thing Mommy did was to give him a bath in lots of water and soap. As we watched, fleas came floating to the top of the water. Mommy soaped and rinsed and soaped and rinsed, and the fleas just kept floating to the top. She finally decided she had most of them and gave Shadow a good final rinse and toweled him off; the towel was covered with fleas. After Shadow was dry we checked him out. We didn't see any fleas until we turned him over on his back, and sure enough there were still a few flitting about on his belly. But he sure felt a lot better and he turned into a really good dog. The flea problem never went away, though Mommy did the best she could to keep them under control.

We had ducks and chickens in Bacolod City. We didn't do well with our first two baby chicks. A veterinarian told Mommy to give each one half of a malaria pill, to get rid of tapeworms. When she did, alas! she not only got rid of the tapeworms but the chicks too. They died six hours later. We were all pretty upset, as you can imagine, especially Mommy, who said she should have known it was a crazy idea. Those chicks were replaced with two others that grew up very well. They weren't anything special, no special breed, but we loved them and they turned into great pets. We could go right up to them and pick them up and they would sit happily in our arms.

In Baguio I had a pet hen I was extremely proud of because she laid double-yoked eggs. To keep her from being stolen, Daddy built a cage for her to live in when I was not playing with her. It was outside my bedroom window, very high off the ground.

We had a number of ducks in Bacolod City and it really upset me when one was stolen. I knew it would be killed and eaten. Our ducks were not in cages and so were easy to steal.

In Bacolod City Peter decided to raise a pig to sell to make money. We also bought twenty chicks to raise, to sell, and to eat. Daddy and Peter made a two-storey pen for Peter's pig and the chickens. The pig was on the bottom of the pen and up above him half-way across the pen was a cage with a wire bottom for the chickens. That way all the chicken poop and the food the chickens dropped went down on the floor of the pig's pen and he ate it. Peter also fed the pig table scraps and pig food and all of us were assigned a day to clean out the pig's pen and feed him. Mommy had the job of feeding the pig the big snails that lived all over our yard, on the banana plants and other trees. About every two weeks Mommy collected the snails, dumped them, in their shells, in a pot of water, and boiled them. Once they cooled down, she dumped them into the pigpen. The pig thought they were delicious and crunched away. We were told that people ate the slimy things as well. I guess if you are hungry, you will eat almost anything.

It was hard seeing that pig sold, because we had made a pet out of him. He loved us to wash him and to scratch his belly, and he would peacefully eat the grass while we sat on him. But when he got big enough, Peter sold him to a neighbor and bought himself a scooter. He was very proud. It reminded us that we shouldn't make a pet out of an animal we would be selling. We did slaughter and eat ten of the chickens and sold the rest.

One of the more unpleasant sights was watching a dead pig being brought into the open market. It had been gutted but still had its head and tail. It was dragged across the muddy walkway to a market stall with a dirt floor and hung on a hook. Customers could buy any part they wanted – the vendor just hacked off a piece. Mommy did not buy pork, ham, or bacon.

The meat market was often smelly, dark, with flies all around, especially on the meat. Even worse was the fish market. Before we got near it, a terrible fish smell floated out in the hot air from under the low ceiling. We only went there once, and Mommy couldn't bring herself to buy any fish. I think it was about the only time I saw something Mommy just couldn't deal with. The only time we had fish was when Delia bought it when she went to market for Mommy. And she had to cook it too; Mommy just couldn't. Every now and then we did eat fish at restaurants and homes we visited. We never did try a special dish made of raw fish that was supposed to be delicious and a favorite everywhere. According to Peace Corps rules, raw fish was forbidden and Mommy believed one hundred per cent in following rules like that. Mommy did buy ground beef now and then, and she cooked it to death and mixed it in with other stuff most of the time, so the flavor was pretty much out of it. The good thing was that while we were in the Philippines, we never got sick from the food or caught one of the diseases that could stay with you for life.

One day, we went to visit a farm Daddy's boss wanted him to see, where President Marcos had some champion Charolais cattle. They were white and large, and I thought they were the prettiest beef cows I had ever seen. Their faces were so gentle looking that you wanted to give them a big hug. The bull, however, didn't look very lovable. He was huge and he was tall, I mean really tall. But he did look noble and handsome. I decided I wanted a herd just like the president's someday. During that trip, we saw baby calves, which licked my fingers with their wet sticky tongues and sent a tickle through me — just like little calves in the States.

The most fun on that trip was riding in a cart being pulled by a very old carabao and then getting to sit on his back. It was a dream come true for me. His hide was gray and dusty, with only a little stiff hair growing on it that tickled my legs. We each had a turn. That carabao just stood there, patient as could be, letting us sit on him. Matthew, though, refused to get on. When we suggested he do so, he just looked at us, stuck his thumb in his mouth, and stood his ground.

The carabao is a water buffalo and we thought they were great. They were everywhere in the Philippines, and for me they were the symbol of the country. The carabao was the most important animal the Filipinos had, especially the farmers. They were used for all types of work, mostly farm work, for milk, and of course, for meat. However, they were not used for meat until they were too old to work. My brothers and I would run out in the fields in our neighborhood with our Filipino friends and watch the farm children sitting on the backs of the carabaos or leading them by the nose with a rope. The farmers made a hole in the carabao's nose, pulled the rope through it and made a knot in it so the rope couldn't come out. I guess it was like piercing a person's ears, except it was a pretty big hole. There weren't any fences, so it was the job of the children to keep the carabaos from roaming away. I thought that would be a great job.

The carabaos loved the mud, and it was fun watching them roll around in it to keep cool and to keep bugs off. When they came up out of the mud, they looked like giant mud statues. Sometimes we would see them out in the field with little white birds following them and jumping on their backs to peck bugs off. We wanted Mommy and Daddy to buy us one, but of course they didn't. Instead we bought lots of wooden statues of them in various sizes. One statue that Daddy bought was about the size of a beagle!

We often saw men carving the statues, using simple tools to do the job. They sat on the ground and often used their bare feet to help hold what they were carving. We went carabao crazy! Our second Christmas we took a family photo with our big wooden carabao in it, front and center.

So while it was different having pets in the Philippines, we certainly had our share of them just as we did in the States. And we also found that pets and other animals act the same whether in America or another country. They all want loving care and will be our friends, if given the chance.

The pig - chicken project

Carabao and calf

Our last photo, with Vicky, as a Peace Corps Family

Going Home

NANCY - 1973

Despite having to adjust to another move, martial law, and the heavy rains, our year in Baguio generally went well. Our schools played a big part in helping us enjoy our last year. It was also easier because we had been in the country for a year and had gotten to know the culture and what to expect. The two cities were also very different and it was neat having the chance to live on two different islands. We noticed immediately that the people in Baguio were more used to foreigners, including Peace Corps Volunteers. When we were in the city, there was a definite decrease in cheek-pinching, giggles, and pointing, and we no longer had groups of people surround or follow us, as had been the case in Bacolod City. Out in the rural areas and small villages, we drew more attention but never on the same scale as in Bacolod City. In Baguio, as in Bacolod City, what did draw people's attention was that we were a family living among them, using public transportation, and being a part of their everyday life. This was different and made us different from other *"Canos."* What Baguio didn't have was colorful, decorated jeepneys; theirs were painted darker colors and were drab in comparison. There weren't any *calesas* either. Even the buses were not as colorful.

Our life in Baguio went along pretty much as it had in Bacolod City. We went to school, played with friends, went to market, did laundry, celebrated birthdays and holidays, and were careful about using water.

We finally found a clean public beach, not far from Baguio, near the town of San Fernando on the west side of Luzon Island. One time we went by bus to the beach and another time Sister Helena lent us the convent's little blue truck, which of course got us to the beach faster. The beach was not crowded, and we had a wonderful time playing and splashing in the waves and finding real live starfish that we could catch and hold.

Before we knew it, there were only three months left of our time with Peace Corps, and our parents started planning for the end of our stay and our return home. It was an up-and-down time for all of us. In some ways, we kids wanted to stay another year, because we loved our schools so much, even Daniel. Daddy also talked about extending for another year, but after some thought we all decided that wasn't what we really wanted to do.

There was a lot to do to get ready to leave. Mommy and Daddy had to talk with our director to see if we could get permission to leave a few months early. We wanted to do some traveling on our way home and get home early enough to allow some adjustment time before school started in September. We also had to plan where we wanted to go on our trip. We finally decided to go camping in five countries in Europe for five weeks, where we would also have the opportunity to see and meet relatives we had in England and friends in Denmark and Holland.

Mommy and Daddy also had to finish up their work. They felt good about what they had accomplished and were encouraged by the fact that, thanks to Sister Helena at the Good Shepherd Convent, what they had started would indeed continue after they left. They thought that they had made a difference in the lives of at least a few people. Then too all the pets had to be placed in good homes and all our things packed for shipping. And we had to say goodbye.

The packing turned out to be a big deal because we were taking back to the States much more than we had brought with us. We had all the carabaos we had collected, along with other wood carvings, and our parents had bought a whole set of dishes carved by hand and serving dishes made out of wood. Then there were wooden wall hangings, paintings, Filipino Christmas decorations, special Filipino clothes, linens and blankets – to name but a few things going home with us. Again, Daddy built a big box for us to put it all in. We also had to go through another medical exam, to make sure we were all healthy and in good shape to return home.

It was hard to believe that it was all just about over and that our lives would change again, as we adjusted to being back in the States. We were going home a different family, because we were all two years older and had lived a very different life in our time away. The experience had a big influence on our growing belief in the dignity and worth of each individual. My brothers and I had done our best to spread goodwill and friendship, and my parents had taken John F. Kennedy's word to heart. "Ask not what your country can do for you; ask what you can do for your country." And, we add, for the world, community, of which we are all a part.

The big day came; on June 30, 1973, we boarded a plane for home. From the window, I saw the islands of the Philippines. I saw the mountains where we had lived in Baguio and thought of the mountainside rice terraces we'd visited and the rain and mudslides we'd endured. I saw miles of flatlands and flat, watery rice fields and remembered planting rice while we were in training. Along some of the rivers running into the ocean, I saw squatters' homes made out of tin and all crammed together, and I remembered our visit to Delia's home. I saw dirty, brown rivers, flowing into the ocean and slowly becoming a part of it and thought of the women and children washing their clothes on the river banks. As we climbed higher, the poverty and life of the islands disappeared. Just before we went into the clouds, the islands appeared as a mixture of beautiful greens and browns, with white sand beaches flowing into the ocean. I couldn't see any dirty beaches, although I knew they were there. Instead I thought of the few times we got to swim and play on clean beaches and in clean ocean waters. From up high, what I saw was the beauty below me, the beautiful things about the Philippines and the things I would miss.

According to my parents, we had been living in a third-world country, a country with too many people, lots of poverty, and lots of problems. I had seen all that and lived within it all, but I also saw beautiful things, and I remember being happy while we lived there, except for my first year at school. That short period of time was less important now, because of my joyful experience at Chefoo School. I wished I could have picked up the school, with its students and teachers, and brought them home with me. I wanted to bring a carabao home too. I knew I would miss jeepneys. I would not miss the hot buses, crowded with people, animals, and things inside and out, that rattled so much that you were sure they were going to fall apart. I would miss the friendly people, but not being followed, pinched, laughed at, or targeted by the rocks some of the kids threw at us. They threw rocks at each other too, so I suppose that was just something they did.

Our plane continued on up, and we were flying in and among beautiful white clouds with just a tinge of gray in them. Every now and then, I would get one more glimpse of the islands. I was sad as I thought of the pets we had to leave behind. A Filipino vet who knew our family took Amiga. He promised he would not eat her, but that didn't help my sadness at leaving her, or prevent a continuing concern about her becoming a meal. What if she was stolen? She would get eaten then. As for my pet hen and the rabbit, I knew that they would become food at some point in time.

Then there was Vicky, the college student who had lived with us in Baguio and gone with us everywhere. Vicky had become a part of our family; it seemed like she should be coming with us. She came with us to Manila to spend our last days together before leaving for home. We all cried when we said goodbye, even my brothers. I wondered if I would ever see her again. She had taken our dog Shadow, and I knew she would take good care of him. Caesar and one of his sisters had also come to see us off in Manila. He had really wanted to come with us; it was his dream to live in the U.S. Mommy said that she would always remember how Caesar took our family under his wing when we lived in Bacolod

City. When we moved, he continued to visit us. He, too, was a part of us. And of course there was Delia, to whom we had said our sad goodbyes in Baguio, when she returned to her family. I will always remember her teaching me how to shine the floor with a coconut husk. She, Vicky, and Caesar had played such big roles in helping us to live in their country as one of them—not on the sidelines, sheltered in the wealthier communities.

Soon all I was able to see below me was a floor of thick, soft-looking clouds. I looked up and saw clear blue sky and the shining sun above me. It was so quiet, so peaceful—a clear, shining space in which to flow from the Philippines back to another world. When the plane came back down through that thick layer of clouds, I was in another life—not yet home, but more like home than the Philippines. We were in Europe, where we camped in five different countries, before finally heading home.

I was ready to go home and I knew Daniel was too. I had missed the United States. I had missed having four seasons and could hardly wait to see snow again. I knew Peter was really looking forward to snow too; the year-round hot weather had made him cranky. I wanted to see the leaves changing colors again, to watch them fluttering down as I threw them up in the air, and to play in piles of fallen leaves. I was ready to smell the difference as the seasons changed from spring to summer and summer to fall. I was ready for our traditional Christmas and Thanksgiving with family and friends and wanted our American Easter and Halloween back.

Most of all, I couldn't wait to get home and get a pony. I was so ready for one; I hoped my parents were. Daddy was going to work for Farm & Wilderness Camps in Plymouth, Vermont, as their farmer. They also wanted him to develop an educational year-round farm. We had lived and worked at the camps before, so we knew exactly what they were like. Daniel and I were excited about living there. I knew there would be room for a pony. I could just picture myself caring for him and riding him across the fields, with my hair flying behind me.

As I thought what would happen next for me—like the pony, for instance, I wondered how Peter and Matthew would do. There were many things that Peter remembered about home and many he had forgotten, but I had a feeling he would adjust very quickly to the camps, since he had been there before. Matthew didn't remember much about home. He didn't know what ovens or vacuum cleaners were. And all he knew about laundry was washing clothes by hand or in the old wringer washer that he had caught his arm in. He didn't remember us having a car, but he sure knew a lot about jeepneys. He even knew how to wave one down. He might miss having bananas and rice to eat every day. I knew he would not miss being pinched on the cheek and touched. Because he was the youngest, and the blondest, he had the worst of it. Matthew would have to learn about living in our own country all over again. I felt sure he would remember Grandma and Grandpa Stone, since they had visited us last Christmas.

The Philippines was a different place, with a different culture, but it hadn't taken us long to find out that kids are kids everywhere. In the Philippines I'd seen children who barely had a house to live in, with hardly any clothes, without enough to eat. And I knew in the United States there were poor children too. What I had learned was that children's experiences were, basically, very similar. We all feel happiness and sadness, have good days and bad days. Kids in happy homes are usually happy; those in unhappy ones, those who are hungry, cold, or sick are unhappy—no matter where they live. And wherever we are, there are mean kids and nice kids. No matter where we live or whether or not you are poor, kids all like to play and learn. And we all want somebody to be there to dry our tears and laugh with us, to praise us for our accomplishments. We want someone to keep us safe and tell us good night. Our cultures might be different, but in those ways we are all the same.

Our Peace Corps journey had started with us leaving the States from Dulles International Airport way back in the beginning of July 1971. We traveled west across our country and the Pacific Ocean to the Philippines.

Two years later at the end of June 1973 we began our return to the States. We left the Philippines and continued traveling west, crossing Europe on our camping trip—where we saw our first snow in the Alps in two years. Before we knew it, we were flying across the Atlantic Ocean, still going west, back to Dulles Airport to be met by our grandparents in warm hugs and greetings that felt really great. We had traveled all the way around the world. That was just awesome! It was quite the trip, and it felt good getting back home to our own country, seeing friends and loved ones and the glorious, green mountains in Vermont, where we would be making our next home.

It was fun, and exciting unpacking all our possessions after two years. Holding my dolls and other precious treasures in my arms once more gave me a feeling of bliss and contentment to be with them once more. I think maybe the funniest part was when we first got home and Matthew walked into his grandparents' house and looked around and in total seriousness asked Mommy, "Why don't they have any bananas?" And the best part—I did get my pony.

Matthew left of the wheel, Nancy to the right,
Daniel standing on the wheel, and Peter under it

EPILOGUE
Where We Are Today

2011

Three years after leaving Peace Corps, we finally fulfilled our dream of owning a farm in Orwell, Vermont, just 20 miles south of Middlebury. We named it Stonewood Farm, and here Daniel, Nancy, Peter, and Matthew finished their growing-up years and education. We bought the farm in October of 1976 as an operational dairy farm and in 1989 started making the change over to turkeys. We now have the largest turkey farm in Vermont—28,000 birds. All four children were married on the farm, two by me, since at the time I was a justice of the peace. All the grandchildren except for one were born in Middlebury/Rutland and lived on the farm for the first few years of their lives.

During the years following Peace Corps, we maintained contact only with Caesar and Vicky. In the mid 1980's, Caesar came to live in the States and visited us for a few days one summer. In 1990's, Vicky and a friend came over to visit relatives. They too spent a few days with us and saw their first real snow. Since then we have lost contact with these two friends who had been so important to us while we were Peace Corps Volunteers.

So what are Daniel, Nancy, Peter and Matthew doing as adults? Here they are to tell you, again in their own words.

Daniel Stone

Everybody calls me Dan now. Except of course my mom or if I'm in trouble!

I graduated from Fair Haven Union High School in Fair Haven, Vermont in 1978. After high school, having had enough of everyone telling me what I needed to study, I went to Castleton State Collage part-time. Along with courses in things I enjoyed, like art, astronomy, and literature I took a course in photography, a hobby of mine since I got my first camera in the Philippines. During this time, I also continued to work on our farm but soon decided that a farmer I was not. What I enjoyed most was the many construction projects we had on the farm, from remodeling to building new farm buildings. I have always enjoyed building things. This led me to enroll in Vermont Technical College to study architecture. I graduated in 1982 with an Associate's Degree in Architectural Design and Building Engineering.

In the fall, I moved to New Haven, Connecticut, where I started my construction career. I worked for a company that built sunrooms for homes and also built custom glass structures. There I met my future wife, and we were married in 1984.

Having always enjoyed Vermont, we moved back and I started a new job with a building contractor, where I soon became a job-site leader, with my own crew to manage. We built all types of projects from homes to barns for dairy farms. However my time in Vermont was soon over, because after a year I was offered a job with a cabinet-maker in Washington, D.C. This appealed to me because I would not only be building cabinets but also designing them. An added appeal was the fact that I had spent my early years in Northern Virginia and my grandparents were all still living there. So once again we moved.

After a few years, I decided to start my own contracting company in Loudoun County, Virginia. I had determined I was not at my best working for somebody else and decided to become my own boss. I had a crew of three to five men, depending on the jobs. We did all types of residential construction, from small additions to whole houses, for building contractors. I started using my design skills and worked with builders and clients to design homes, using the abilities learned in college.

In 1989, our son Jesse was born, and I decided it was time we had our own home which I planned on building. In 1990, we purchased a one-acre lot in Jefferson County, West Virginia. It is close to Harpers Ferry and walking distance from the Shenandoah River. I believe that my experience in the Philippines influenced the way we built our home. Much of it is built from salvaged, used, left-over, collected, and handmade materials. The end result was different though. It is an attractive, comfortable, well designed house, not at all like the bare structures the poor in the Philippines would stick together out of anything they could find. About two years later, with lots of help from friends and family, our house was finished enough for us to move in, but the "finishing" and changes continue to this day.

In 1993, when the local economy was not so good, I went to work for a company that installed interior trim and custom-built cabinetry. Here I found again that the craftsmanship of cabinet-making and the designing of interior trim and its application were what I most enjoyed doing. After three years, the owner asked if I wanted to take over the company and I purchased it, starting again to work for myself. I have been working with builders, architects, and home-owners ever since, designing, building and installing interior trim, cabinetry, and millwork.

My time in the Philippines has affected the way I look at our world and the people in it. At times it causes personal struggles, since I work with relatively wealthy customers and remain so aware of the poverty that exists in places like the Philippines and even in our own country. It is just not right for so few to have so much and so many to have so very little. But even though so many of the people I knew and played with in the Philippines were very poor, they still enjoyed life. This knowledge, these memories have really helped me to understand the importance of appreciating simple and small things in life—like people, family, nature, and our earth. It has also taught me that people—no matter how different, poor or rich—are all just human beings trying as best we can to live our lives here on earth. Maybe if more kids could go on a grand adventure like I did with my brothers and sister, the world would be a better place for all.

Peace, Dan

Nancy Stone (Pecor)

First I am a woman. Not a wife or a mother or a career. I am a woman who has been shaped by her parents, extended family, education, and life experiences. I lived in different states and abroad as a child, as my parents believed that "a rolling stone gathers no moss." So we, "the four pebbles" rolled right along with them on their travels. In my heart, since I was a child, I have had three loves: writing, horses, and teaching. And somehow over the course of my life I have managed to combine all three in some very unique ways. I graduated from Mount Holyoke College with my BA in Psychology and Education. After graduation, I became an elementary school teacher. In the 1980's, I taught at Burgundy Farm Country Day School in Alexandria, Virginia; my grandparents were founders of the school in 1946. After three years, I joined the public school system and taught in Arlington, Virginia and later in Vermont.

As a teacher, I often wrote my own curriculum to use in the classroom: integrating units on snakes, colonial times, agriculture, and poetry. Since I come from a long line of innovative educators on both sides of the family, it made perfect sense for my mom and me to combine our skills and knowledge to create and run a camp on Stonewood Farm (the family farm in Vermont) that gave children the opportunity to experience life and work with a family on a real farm. In my late 20's, I went back to school to Meredith Manor Equestrian Centre where I fell in love with the art and sport of dressage. It was there that I combined my love of horses with education, working on my Master's degree in Education with an Emphasis in Equestrian Studies. I ended up teaching at Meredith Manor for 6 years. I moved back to Vermont and met my husband, Sean Pecor, the old-fashioned way, on-line! (This was after beginning to think that I would never find the "right guy" and have children.) We are blessed with two daughters, Moira and Chloe. Seeking warmer weather, we moved to Virginia in 2004, where I started a horse boarding, training, and lesson facility, with the help of my husband. In 2009, we moved to Apex, North Carolina, where we currently live. I recently purchased a very talented Lusitano horse from Brazil, who is helping me realize my dream of becoming an upper-level dressage rider. I volunteer in my daughters' schools, where qualified assistants in the classroom are sorely needed and highly valued. I am a wife and a mother. I wear my different career hats of writing, teaching, and working with horses. I am a woman still becoming.

Peter Stone

One of the most important things that happened in my life was my parents buying our farm. I struggled with my education all the way through high school and know that it was my parents' support and encouragement that got me through. They also instilled in me their love of books and knowledge, so that as an adult, books have become one of my resources for further learning and enjoyment.

But the farm was to become my on-site educational tool—the place where I would learn carpentry skills, farm mechanics, caring for and raising farm animals, and working the land. It was here I would find my work and home. After high school, I worked in construction for about ten years, helping to build homes for families in and around Orwell, Vermont. During that time, I continued to help on the farm as needed.

I came back to the farm full time in the middle 1990's, married Siegrid Mertens, a veterinarian from Brazil, who had come to the States to specialize in the reproduction of dairy cows. We have three children: Nathan, Patrick, and Catherine. In 2009, my parents sold the business part of the farm to Siegrid and me. This involves the raising, slaughtering, and marketing of turkeys and making hay to sell. They have retained the land and buildings, which I rent from them. My parents have remained on the farm, both still being a vital part of it, for which I am grateful and appreciative.

I know that my best school year ever was at Chefoo School in Baguio in the Philippines. That and the educational opportunity to be in Peace Corps as part of my growing up, I will always appreciate.

Matthew Stone

In 1987, I graduated from Middlebury Union High School in Vermont. I went on to graduate from Johnson State College in 1991 with a BA in Theater. While working in theater, I traveled to Houston, Texas, New Haven Connecticut, Philadelphia, and New York City. While in New York, I worked on television shows, such as "Saturday Night Live," and had a chance to work in Lincoln Center, as well. While working in Philadelphia, I met my wife and married in 1994. After leaving the theater in 1996, Sarah and I moved back to Vermont to join the family farm and started our family. After seven years of farming, and with our children Emily and Michael, we moved to St. Augustine, Florida to be closer to Sarah's family. While there I was self-employed as a trim carpenter and became a professional fire fighter, as a way to reach out and serve my community.

Once again, five years later we moved back to Vermont. This time it was to Middlebury, only half an hour from the farm, where our ties to the farm and family were still strong. I also designed and built my own super-insulated home using new materials, and two solid wood doors and an oak counter top from the farm house that had been saved when it was remodeled. All the trim was done with white pine that had been harvested from the farm's woodland. I am presently the Technical Director for the Middlebury Town Hall Theater. I joined the Middlebury Volunteer Fire Department and the heavy rescue unit of the Middlebury Rescue Squad to continue my commitment of serving my community. So one circle has closed, is there yet another?

11378242R00109

Made in the USA
Charleston, SC
20 February 2012